THE BOOK
PARIS

THE BOOK LOVER'S GUIDE TO
PARIS

EMILY COPE

WHITE OWL
AN IMPRINT OF PEN & SWORD BOOKS LTD.
YORKSHIRE – PHILADELPHIA

First published in Great Britain in 2022 by
White Owl
An imprint of
Pen & Sword Books Ltd
Yorkshire - Philadelphia

ISBN 978 1 39900 191 5

A CIP catalogue record for this book is available from the
British Library.

Printed and bound by Short Run Press Limited, Exeter.
Design: SJmagic DESIGN SERVICES, India.

Pen & Sword Books Ltd incorporates the imprints of
Pen & Sword Books Archaeology, Atlas, Aviation, Battleground,
Discovery, Family History, History, Maritime, Military, Naval,
Politics, Railways, Select, Transport, True Crime, Fiction,
Frontline Books, Leo Cooper, Praetorian Press, Seaforth
Publishing, Wharncliffe and White Owl.

For a complete list of Pen & Sword titles please contact

PEN & SWORD BOOKS LIMITED
47 Church Street, Barnsley, South Yorkshire, S70 2AS, England
E-mail: enquiries@pen-and-sword.co.uk
Website: www.pen-and-sword.co.uk

or

PEN AND SWORD BOOKS
1950 Lawrence Rd, Havertown, PA 19083, USA
E-mail: Uspen-and-sword@casematepublishers.com
Website: www.penandswordbooks.com

CONTENTS

PREFACE

WRITING this guidebook has been a real labour of love, if not a daunting one. While I've trodden the boulevards of Paris countless times, the thought of condensing the immense literary significance of this incredible city into a single pocket book was a formidable challenge – but one I was determined to pull off.

Armed with nothing but my wits, a notepad and pen, I spent my days hopping between the many places that still bear the traces of Paris' literary history, collecting as much information as possible and chatting to anyone and everyone who would speak to me (while enjoying a few café allongés along the way). Then, like the many writers who have come before me, I sat down at my little writing desk in my Parisian apartment and got to work.

My aim was to create a concise and colourful guidebook that would not just inform but inspire. Fuelled solely on bread, cheese and wine, I did not stop until I felt that I'd not only done the city justice, but also the hundreds of writers who have called it either home or muse, or both.

For those of you who adore novels as much as the writers who penned them, this book is for you. I hope it will be your guide and companion to the moveable feast that is Paris.

ACKNOWLEDGEMENTS

THANK you to everyone who made this book possible, from the cafés, restaurants, libraries and bookshops who provided some incredible images and stories of their past patrons, to my trusty sidekick and cameraman, Christopher Peilow. And lastly, thank you to the city itself – may you continue to inspire writers everywhere.

INTRODUCTION: PARIS, A LITERARY JUNGLE

"If you are lucky enough to have lived in Paris as a young man, then wherever you go for the rest of your life it stays with you, for Paris is a moveable feast."

Ernest Hemingway, *A Moveable Feast,* **1964**

The relationship between Paris and literature has been nothing short of a passionate love affair. Countless novels, novellas, poems and plays have been penned in or about the City of Light, from timeless tales such as Victor Hugo's

Traditional bouquinistes lining the River Seine. Benh Lieu Song

Les Misérables, to Françoise Sagan's scandalous *A Certain Smile*, modern day bestsellers and everything inbetween.

While writers and artists the world over have made Paris their home, the city has also spawned many of its own indigenous writers – the likes of Colette, Simone de Beauvoir and Émile Zola – and each one of them has left a lasting mark on the city in some way or another.

Starting at the turn of the eighteenth century and taking you all the way through to the present day, whether you want to discover the best bouquinistes, enjoy a night at Oscar Wilde's favourite hotel, or take a drink at the Parisian hideouts that inspired Ernest Hemingway, The Book Lover's Guide to Paris has got everything a budding bibliophile could ever need.

Writers and artists have been leaving their mark on the city for centuries. © Chris Peilow

River Seine. © Amy Murell

© Chris Peilow

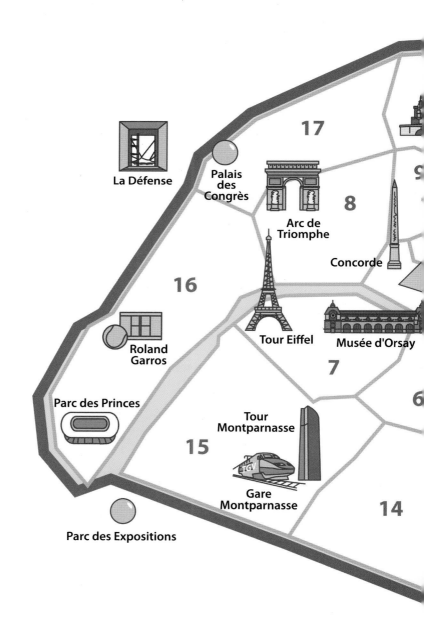

La Défense

Palais des Congrès

17

Arc de Triomphe

8

9

Concorde

16

Roland Garros

Tour Eiffel

Musée d'Orsay

7

Parc des Princes

6

Tour Montparnasse

15

Gare Montparnasse

14

Parc des Expositions

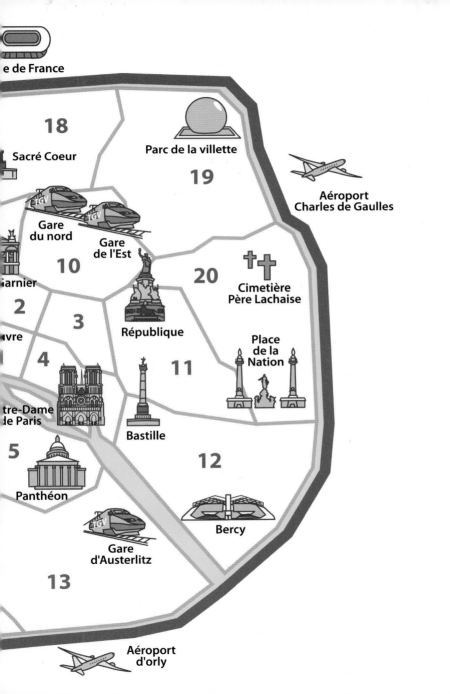

1

VICTOR HUGO'S PARIS

"To breathe Paris is to preserve one's soul"
Victor Hugo, *Les Misérables*, 1862

One of the most celebrated writers in history, Victor Hugo (1802–1885) published an impressive 8 novels, 18 volumes of poetry and 11 plays during his lifetime. Though he is regarded in France as one of the country's greatest poets, he is perhaps best known elsewhere for his novels, *Notre-Dame de Paris* (1831; *The Hunchback of Notre-Dame*) and *Les Misérables* (1862).

Born in Besançon, France, in 1802, Hugo spent many years living and writing in Paris, where he quickly became known for his literary prowess as much as his politics (he was an impassioned campaigner for social justice, which would later become a main theme of his novel *Les Misérables*).

So passionate was Hugo that in 1851 he denounced Louis-Napoléon (Napoleon III) a traitor for seizing complete power and establishing an anti-parliamentary constitution. The incendiary remarks rendered him unwelcome in his own country, and so Hugo fled Paris for Brussels, then took refuge on British territory in Jersey. He remained there from 1852 to 1855, before moving to the neighbouring island of Guernsey, where he stayed until Napoleon III's reign came to an end in 1870.

Far from laying idle during his 20 years in exile (some of which was self-imposed), Hugo continued to pen many works of fiction while apart from his beloved Paris. The detailed and colourful descriptions of the city seen in his novels are testament to how enamoured Hugo was with the capital, a love that prevailed until his eventual return.

Thanks to the controversial urban planner Baron Georges-Eugène Haussmann, many of the medieval streets and hidden slums that Hugo knew and loved have long since disappeared. However it is still possible for travellers to find echoes of Hugo's Paris, from his own home in Place de Vosges to the world-famous cathedral which inspired the author's most enduring novel.

The exterior of Maison de Victor Hugo at Place de Vosges. © Chris Peilow

Maison de Victor Hugo

6 Place des Vosges, 75004
+33 (0) 1 42 72 10 16
maisonsvictorhugo.paris.fr
Metro: Bastille, Saint-Paul, Chemin Vert

Perhaps the first stop for any Hugophile is the writer's home-turned-museum. Situated at the prestigious Place de Vosges in the heart of the Marais district, the writer lived here from 1832 to 1848 with his wife Adèle and their four children.

Since re-named Maison de Victor Hugo, it was here that Hugo wrote a large body of his major works, including a portion of *Les Misérables*, which he started in 1845. Interestingly, multiple sources state that, so as not to procrastinate while writing, Hugo would remove his clothes and give them to his servants with instructions not to return them until he'd finished a chapter.

In her memoirs, Hugo's wife even wrote that during the writing of *The Hunchback of Notre Dame* the author "[purchased] a bottle of ink and a huge grey knitted shawl, which swathed him from head to foot, locked his formal clothes away so that he would not be tempted to go out and entered his novel as if it were a prison."

Hugo was known for his love of interior design, as seen in the Chinese room at Maison de Victor Hugo.
© Pierre Antoine

The red bedroom is a faithful recreation of the bedroom at 130 avenue d'Eylau, where Victor Hugo spent the last seven years of his life. © Pierre Antoine

The museum offers a fascinating insight into the writer's working habits and daily life, containing hundreds of his drawings, manuscripts and his original furniture (including his famous raised desk), as well as authentic reconstructions of his bedroom, study, red room and Chinese living room, which are excellent examples of Hugo's penchant for vibrant interior design.

Did you know? Hugo loved to throw dinner parties, often hosting 30 people a night at his apartment. Fellow French author Alexandre Dumas was also a regular visitor to 6 Place des Vosges during the 1800s.

Le Grand Véfour

17 Rue de Beaujolais, 75001
+33 (0) 1 42 96 56 27
grand-vefour.com/en
Metro: Pyramides, Palais Royal-Musée du Louvre

One of Hugo's favourite spots to eat was Le Grand Véfour in the Palais-Royal, which first opened its doors

Le Grand Véfour has been the finest gourmet rendezvous of Parisian political, artistic and literary society for more than 200 years. © Pascal Soulagnet

in 1784 – though back then it was called Café de Chartres. For many years the restaurant served as a hangout for the political, artistic and literary elite, and the names of its famous patrons are still archived to each table, including the likes of Napoleon, Jean Cocteau and Colette (who lived next door).

Despite being a regular patron, Hugo's order was always the same: *vermicelle, poitrine de mouton et haricots blancs* (vermicelli noodles, mutton and white beans). The menu has since changed, but the restaurant's gilded golden frames, neoclassical paintings, mirrored walls and carved panelling with Louis XVI-style garlands are all original, giving it an authentic grand Parisian feel.

Due to the restaurant's history and Michelin star food – think duck foie gras terrine, crispy frog legs braised with blackcurrant pepper, and Prince Rainier III pigeon – prices are high, but if you're stopping by for lunch or dinner make sure to reserve a seat at the 'Hugo table' with its unbeatable courtyard view.

Interior of Le Grand Véfour. © Pascal Soulagnet

Avenue Victor-Hugo

Metro: Victor Hugo

On his return from exile Hugo was hailed as a national hero by the French people. To show the extent of their adoration, Avenue d'Eylau – where Hugo's last residence was at no. 130 – was renamed Avenue Victor-Hugo in 1881. Hugo's building was demolished in 1907, but above the door at the re-built site (since

Fonquergne sculpture of Victor Hugo above the entrance of 124 Avenue Victor-Hugo, built on the site of no. 130, Hugo's last residence. © Chris Peilow

renumbered no. 124) is a mask of the writer by the sculptor Fonquergne.

That same year, on 27 June, one of the greatest parades in French history was held in the writer's honour. Marchers stretched from the Avenue d'Eylau down the Champs-Élysées, and all the way back to the centre of Paris, as Hugo sat by his window and watched. Many of the official guides even wore cornflowers as a nod to the character Fantine in *Les Misérables*.

Did you know? Since the creation of Avenue Victor-Hugo, letters addressed to the author during the remainder of his life were often labelled: "To Mister Victor Hugo, In his avenue, Paris".

Le Panthéon

Place du Panthéon, 75005
+33 (0) 1 44 32 18 00
paris-pantheon.fr
Metro: Cardinal Lemoine

When Hugo died on 22 May 1885 at the age of 83, he was mourned heavily by the people of France. Not only was he revered as a towering literary giant and a formidable political figure, but he remained a defender of liberty, equality and fraternity until his final breath.

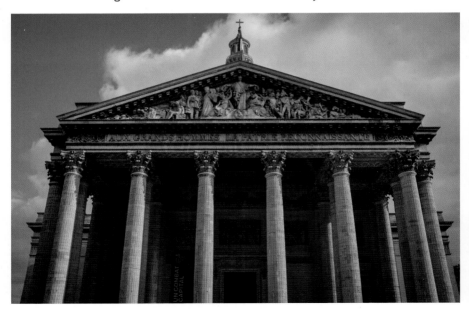

Victor Hugo is buried in the Panthéon's crypt alongside Alexandre Dumas and Émile Zola, as well as Jean-Jacque Rousseau, Marie Curie and Voltaire. © Chris Peilow

Though he had requested a pauper's funeral, Hugo was awarded a state funeral by decree of President Jules Grévy. On 1 June more than two million people joined Hugo's funeral procession as it travelled from the Arc de Triomphe to the Panthéon, where he was laid to rest.

Hugo remains in the crypt beneath the historic building to this day, alongside fellow writers Alexandre Dumas and Émile Zola, as well as Jean-Jacques Rousseau, Marie Curie and Voltaire. If you fancy venturing inside, tours at Le Panthéon run daily from 10am–6pm and audio guides are available to purchase.

Did you know? Most large French towns and cities have a street or square named after Hugo.

The Hunchback of Notre-Dame

Published in 1831 when Hugo was 31 years old, *The Hunchback of Notre-Dame* (or *Notre-Dame de Paris*) is set in a vividly imagined medieval Paris and, though it has since been turned into a Disney film, the original is far from child-friendly.

The sweeping melodrama tells the story of a beautiful gypsy named Esmeralda who is loved by three men: Captain Phoebus, Archdeacon Frollo and his adoptive son Quasimodo, the deformed bellringer of the great Notre-Dame Cathedral.

It seems unbelievable now, but before Hugo's book was published most Parisians saw Notre-Dame as a shabby, outdated antiquity. At the

The world-famous gargoyles of Notre-Dame Cathedral look out across the city. Jawed Karim

time many French Gothic structures were being torn down and replaced by more modern buildings or 'upgraded' with renovations and replacements, but Hugo viewed such destruction as a travesty.

Always one to stand firmly by his beliefs, Hugo set out to make his contemporaries aware of the value of these architectural feats and, most notably, the Notre-Dame Cathedral. Thankfully, Hugo's plan worked.

Both the captivating and tragic story of Esmeralda and Quasimodo, as well as Hugo's impassioned writing about the elegance and importance of the Notre-Dame, drew thousands to the Îsle de la Cité and helped make the cathedral the world-renowned icon it is today.

Cathédrale Notre-Dame de Paris

**6 Parvis Notre-Dame,
Place Jean-Paul II, 75004
notredamedeparis.fr
Metro: Cité, Saint-Michel**

"Great edifices, like great mountains, are the work of centuries"
Victor Hugo, *The Hunchback of Notre-Dame*, 1831

Notre-Dame remains one of the finest examples of French Gothic architecture in the country and is extremely popular

The façade of Notre-Dame Cathedral is a remarkable feat of Gothic architecture.
Madhurantakam

A front view of the Notre-Dame Cathedral. © Chris Peilow

with tourists. Visitors from across the globe flock to the Île de la Cité to view the enormous cathedral and its impressive Gothic bell towers, snarling gargoyles, flying buttresses and colourful rose windows.

Notre-Dame's three pipe organs and immense church bells (which Quasimodo was in charge of ringing) are amoung some of the most precious artefacts inside the building, while many historical events have taken place at the cathedral, including the coronation of Napoleon I; The Allied liberation of Paris in 1944 was also celebrated at Notre-Dame with the singing of the Magnificat.

Sadly, during the fire of 2019, the oak roof beams supporting the lead roof were destroyed and the main spire collapsed. However, restoration work is underway and Notre-Dame offers free, hour-long tours of the exterior every day, providing information on its history, architecture and more.

The Court of Miracles

"A gutter of vice and beggary, of vagrancy that spills over into the streets of the capital... an immense changing-room of all the actors of his comedy that robbery, prostitution and murder play on the cobbled streets of Paris"

Victor Hugo, *The Hunchback of Notre-Dame*, 1831

Immortalised in *The Hunchback of Notre-Dame*, the Court of Miracles (*Cour de Miracles*) was based on a very real place.

Gustave Doré's illustration of the Court of Miracles in Victor Hugo's novel, **Notre-Dame de Paris c.1860.**

During the reign of King Louis XIV, from 1643 to 1715, the poor population of Paris ballooned, leading to slums which housed prostitutes, beggars, thieves and many of the city's homeless. A society unto themselves, within these slums there was an intricate system of laws, rites of passage to enter, and many groups had their own leaders and languages.

The most unfortunate of this downtrodden lot relied on begging to survive. In order to garner sympathy in the hope of more charitable donations, beggars would often wear disguises to make themselves appear physically disabled or diseased.

Come nightfall, when the poor returned home to the slums, there was no need to feign illness and so, stripped of their ailments, they appeared miraculously recovered – hence, the Court of Miracles.

To find what remains of one such slum, head down Rue d'Aboukir in the 2nd arrondissement and look out for Rue de Damiette. There, a plaque marks the location of the Court of Miracles, though there were many more dotted around central Paris.

Les Misérables

Since the day of its publication in April 1862, *Les Misérables* has remained at the forefront of bestseller lists across the globe. Thought to be one of the greatest novels ever written (as well as one of the longest, with the original coming in at 655,478 words), *Les Misérables* has been translated into more than 22 different languages, adapted numerous times for TV and film, and is the third longest-running musical in Broadway history.

Hugo first started working on the novel in 1845 at the age of 43, and continued to toil with his masterpiece during political exile in Guernsey. Goaded on by his Belgian publisher, Albert Lacroix, Hugo finally finished the hefty novel 17 years later.

A tale of injustice, heroism and love, *Les Misérables* follows protagonist Jean Valjean – an ex-convict who spent 19 years in prison for stealing a loaf of bread – as he tries to make an honest man of himself. The action begins in 1815 and follows events over the next two decades, including the Paris Uprising of 1832, and presents the vast panorama of Parisian society, from the heights of the aristocracy to the underworld of Parisian prostitutes, beggars and criminals.

Ultimately, Hugo uses his novel to trace the social impact of the numerous revolutions, insurrections and executions taking place at the time, as well as condemning the unjust class-based structure of nineteenth-century France, casting an especially critical eye on criminal justice, education and the treatment of women.

Despite being set nearly 200 years ago, numerous locations featured in the novel can still be visited and enjoyed across Paris to this day.

Jardin du Luxembourg

Rue de Vaugirard, 75006
+33 (0) 1 42 64 33 99
senat.fr/visite/jardin
Metro: Odéon

"One day, the air was warm, the Luxembourg was inundated with light and shade, the sky was as pure as though the angels had washed it that morning, the sparrows were giving vent to little twitters in the depths of the chestnut-trees."

Victor Hugo, *Les Misérables*,1862

Just south of Luxembourg Palace (where the French Senate meets) lies the Jardin du Luxembourg. Created in the early 1600s by Marie de Medici and modelled after parks in her native Florence, it is in this garden that the principal love story of *Les Misérables* unfolds when the characters Marius Pontmercy and Cosette first meet.

From the moment they lock eyes, Marius falls head over heels in love and journeys to the gardens everyday to sit on a bench and pretend to read as he

A total of 106 sculptures are dotted throughout the Jardin du Luxembourg. © Chris Peilow

The Luxembourg Palace. © Chris Peilow

waits for Cosette and Valjean to walk past during their daily strolls.

With its 23 hectares of lawns, tree-lined promenades and 106 sculptures dotted throughout the grounds, it's easy to see why Hugo was so inspired by the place. In fact, Hugo was just one of many writers to appreciate the Jardin du Luxembourg's charms, with Charles Baudelaire, Jean-Paul Sartre, Honoré de Balzac and Ernest Hemingway also being frequent guests during their respective time periods.

The gardens feature an orchard which houses a variety of old and forgotten apple strains, an apiary for visitors to learn about bee-keeping, the monumental Medici fountain, chess sets and pétanque courts, as well as many activities and facilities for children, including puppet shows, rides, slides and remote-control boats.

Traveller's tip: Keep an eye out for the bronze model of the Statue of Liberty on the west side of the gardens, which was sculpted by Auguste Bartholdi, the same man who created the full-sized Statue of Liberty in New York.

Musée des Égouts de Paris

Face au 93 Quai d'Orsay, 75001
+33 (0) 1 53 68 27 81
paris.fr/equipements
** musee-des-egouts-5059**
Metro: Alma-Marceau

"The great prodigality of Paris, her marvellous fête, her Beaujon folly, her orgy, her full-handed outpouring of gold, her pageant, her luxury, her magnificence, is her sewer"

Victor Hugo,
Les Misérables, 1962

The Musée des Égouts (Sewer Museum), located in the sewers beneath the Quai d'Orsay on the Left Bank, is one of the most fascinating museums in Paris and offers some incredible insights into the city's unique history.

Sewers have been draining wastewater in Paris since the beginning of the thirteenth century, when the first underground system was constructed under Rue Montmartre by order of King Phillipe II. However, it wasn't until the reign of Napoleon Bonaparte that covered sewers were introduced and the construction of today's network of more than 1,312 miles of sewer tunnels began in 1850 – though it wasn't initially this large and has been expanding to encompass the growing capital ever since.

It is within these subterranean sewers that *Les Misérables'* hero, Valjean, flees the barricade with a wounded Marius on his back, before being accosted by Inspector Javert. Hugo saw the sewers of Paris as a place where class distinctions became insignificant, which is perhaps why he chose to set one of the novel's most climactic scenes within the rat run of tunnels.

The museum is open most days and offers tours chronicling the sewer system's modern developments, as well as information and exhibits on the history and engineering of the tunnels, making it the perfect place to retrace Valjean's steps.

Saint-Paul-Saint-Louis Church

99 Rue Saint-Antoine, 75004
+33 (0) 1 42 72 30 32
spsl.fr
Metro: Saint-Paul

"People halted in the Rue Saint-Antoine, in front of Saint-Paul, to gaze through the windows of the carriage at the orange-flowers quivering on Cosette's head"
Victor Hugo,
Les Misérables, 1862

Located in the Marais neighbourhood, this Baroque church serves as the setting for the wedding of Marius and Cosette at the end of Hugo's masterpiece. Having lived nearby in Place des Vosges, Hugo was a parishioner of the church and donated the shell-shaped holy water fonts on either side of the entrance. Perhaps not by coincidence, Hugo's daughter Léopoldine was also married in the church in 1843.

Constructed between 1627 and 1641 by the Jesuits with the financial aid of Louis XIII, Saint-Paul-Saint-Louis Church was the first church to completely break away from the Gothic tradition. With many fascinating features, such as an immense dome, Baroque stained-glass windows, a grandstand organ and the signature of Hugo preserved in the parish registers, Saint-Paul-Saint-Louis Church is certainly worth a visit.

The church also hosts tours and holds mass almost daily, but make sure to check the website for up-to-date schedules.

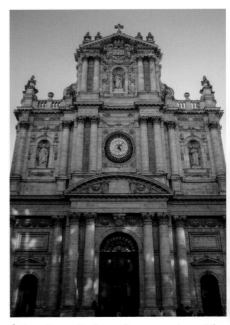

Église Saint-Paul-Saint-Louis serves as the wedding venue for Marius and Cosette in **Les Misérables.**
© Chris Peilow

2

GREAT FRENCH WRITERS OF THE NINETEENTH CENTURY

Despite his weighty reputation and enduring legacy, Hugo wasn't the only great French writer of the nineteenth century. In fact, during this period France enjoyed enormous international literary prestige, with the likes of Honoré de Balzac, George Sand, Alfred de Musset and many more producing an impressive body of work.

A truly fascinating period in French history, the nineteenth century saw the rise of democracy and the end of monarchy and empire in France, and spanned the political regimes of Napoleon Bonaparte's Consulate (1799–1804) and Empire (1804–1814), the Restoration under Louis XVII and Charles X (1814–1830), the July Monarchy under Louis Philippe d'Orléans (1830–1848), and the first decades of the Third Republic (1871–1940).

Such huge cultural and political changes and their effect on society are reflected in the many classic works which were penned during this century, with writers beginning to explore and experiment with different literary themes and styles, such as romanticism, realism and naturalism, while grappling to make sense of such turbulent times.

Honoré de Balzac

Honoré de Balzac (1799–1850) penned his multi-volume novel sequence, *La Comédie Humaine* (1834; *The Human Comedy*) while living in Paris. The work, which presents a panorama of post-Napoleonic French life, is generally viewed as his magnum opus.

Like many of the great creatives, Balzac's work habits were legendary. In his own description, written in March 1833, Balzac said of his punishing schedule:

"I go to bed at six or seven in the evening, like the chickens; I'm waked at one o'clock in the morning, and I work until eight;

at eight I sleep again for an hour and a half; then I take a little something, a cup of black coffee, and go back into my harness until four. I receive guests, I take a bath, and I go out, and after dinner I go to bed. I'll have to lead this life for some months, not to let myself be snowed under by my debts."

Maison de Balzac is one the 14 City of Paris museums. © Myriam Legras

Balzac's *oeuvre* includes *La Cousine Bette* (1846; *Cousin Bette*), *Ursule Mirouët* (1842), and *Eugenie Grandet* (1833), as well as many plays, short stories and novellas. He influenced countless famous writers, including the novelists Émile Zola, Charles Dickens, Gustave Flaubert and Henry James, as well as filmmaker François Truffaut, and philosophers such as Friedrich Engels and Karl Marx, while also helping to establish the traditional form of the novel.

It is no exaggeration to say that, without Balzac, literature today would be very different.

Maison de Balzac

47 Rue Raynouard, 75016
+33 (0) 1 55 74 41 80
en.parisinfo.com/paris-museum-
    monument/71078/Maison-de-Balzac
Metro: Passy

Standing in the heart of the old Passy village, it was in this house that *La Comédie Humaine* came to life. The museum exhibits numerous original editions, manuscripts and illustrations of Balzac's works, as well as the writer's paintings, engravings and personal memoirs, and some fascinating memorabilia and curios from his life (including his rather grand turquoise cane).

One of the 14 City of Paris museums, Maison de Balzac is a must-see for fans of the author.

Traveller's tip: Make sure to check the website before visiting as the museum regularly organises exhibitions and events on themes relating to the writer.

Balzac's writing desk at the Maison de Balzac. © Raphaël Chipault

Monument to Balzac

77 Rue de Varenne, 75007
+33 1(0) 44 18 61 10
musee-rodin.fr
Metro: Varenne, Invalides

The Monument to Balzac is a sculpture created by Auguste Rodin in memory of the French novelist. Commissioned by Société des Gens de Lettres in 1891 – 41 years after the

Rodin first conceived The Thinker as part of his work The Gates of Hell. They are both on display at the Rodin Museum. Tammy Lo

The Monument de Balzac in the grounds of the Rodin Museum. Beyond My Ken

writer's death – Rodin worked on the project for eight years and used living lookalikes and all the images he could find to capture the writer's likeness and spirit.

By the end of his commission Rodin had made a large number of studies, ranging from Balzac dressed in a monk's habit to a completely naked figure. His final choice, showing Balzac in his dressing gown, displeased the Société des Gens de Lettres so much they rejected it. The patinated plaster cast which was used to make the final bronze statue is now on display at Musée Rodin, as is the bronze statue itself (when not on loan).

Traveller's tip: Entry to Musée Rodin costs €13 and visitors can also see more works of the French sculptor, including The Thinker, The Kiss and The Gates of Hell.

George Sand

During the mid-nineteenth century George Sand (1804–1876) was more renowned in England than both Hugo and Balzac, which was no small feat at the time given that she was a woman.

A fascinating and somewhat trailblazing figure both in literature and society, Sand was known to her friends and family as Aurore and spent much of her childhood being raised by her grandmother, Marie-Aurore de Saxe, in the French province of Berry – a beloved setting she used in many of her later rustic novels.

In 1831 Sand moved to Paris and published her first solo novel, *Indiana* (1832), under the pseudonym George Sand. The work explored female desire as well as the class and social constraints which bound a woman to her husband (under the Napoleonic Code women could not obtain property, claim ownership of their children or divorce).

On publication Sand found immediate success, thrusting her firmly into the limelight and finally bringing a much-needed female voice to the French literary canon. But it wasn't solely Sand's writing talents that turned heads.

In 1800 the police issued an order requiring women to apply for a permit to wear 'male' clothing (including trousers, waistcoats, frock coats and hats). However, Sand continued to wear such attire without applying for a permit – her justification being that 'male' clothing was less expensive, more comfortable and sturdier than the typical dress of a noblewoman. Equally scandalous was Sand's insistence on smoking a tobacco pipe in public, which was greatly frowned upon if you were a woman.

Musée de la Vie Romantique

16 Rue Chaptal, 75009
+33 (0) 55 31 95 67
en.parisinfo.com/paris-museum-
    monument/71482/Musee-de-la-Vie-
    romantique
Metro: Pigalle, Blanche

If you're interested in learning more about Sand and her fascinating life and literature, then the Musée de la Vie Romantique is an essential stop on your Parisian tour. While the museum itself resides in the former house of painter Ary Scheffer, three of the rooms on the ground floor are dedicated to Sand, exhibiting portraits of her relatives, as well as pieces of the author's furniture and jewellery, her drawings and writing.

In reality, Sand lived a short walk away in the Square d'Orléans (there's a plaque commemorating her residence), though it is believed that the writer visited Scheffer during his Friday evening salons – often accompanied by her lover, composer Frédéric Chopin.

The Musée de la Vie Romantique (Museum of Romantic Life) housed in the Scheffer-Renan mansion. Myrabella

Café Procope

13 Rue de l'Ancienne Comédie, 75006
+33 (0) 40 46 79 00
procope.com/en
Metro: Mabillon

Thought to be the oldest café in Paris, Café Procope was founded in 1686 by Sicilian chef Francesco Procopio dei Coltelli and became a major literary and philosophical hotspot during the eighteenth and nineteenth century.

Used as a meeting place for notable figures such as Voltaire and American statesmen Thomas Jefferson and Benjamin Franklin, the café was also regularly frequented by Sand at the height of her writing career.

The café has since been refurbished to mimic the old eighteenth century style and now attracts more tourists than literary greats, but it's still well worth a look in – if not just

Café Procope serves traditional French cuisine such as coq au vin, snails and steak. Jean-Marie Hullot

for a cup of their famous *chocolat chaud*.

Did you know? Denis Diderot is said to have written parts of the *Encyclopédie* while dining at Café Procope.

Alexandre Dumas

Known for his novels depicting swashbuckling high adventure, justice and vengeance, such as *Le Comte de Monte-Cristo* (1844; *The Count of Monte Cristo*) and *Le Prince des Voleurs* (1872; *The Prince of Thieves*), it is perhaps the adventures of D'Artagnan and the three musketeers which remains Alexandre Dumas' (1802–1870) best-loved creation.

Born in Villers-Cotterêts in Northern France, Dumas moved to Paris in 1822 where he built his reputation first as a playwright and then as a historical novelist. As with many successful authors at the time, after gaining notoriety Dumas indulged his extravagant tastes in food, drink and women, and was consequently forced to produce increasing amounts of fiction in order to pay his creditors.

Alexandre Dumas. J. Paul Getty Museum

Throughout his career Dumas was assisted in his writing by ghostwriter, Auguste Maquet, a trained historian. The duo were a collaborative team for nearly 20 years and it is generally believed that Maquet researched history, outlined plots and sketched characters, while Dumas embellished on Maquet's research with his trademark swift action and clever dialogue.

In addition to his money problems, Dumas often faced discrimination due to his mixed race heritage – his grandmother, born in Haiti, was a black slave and he used her name rather than his father's title of Marquis Davy de la Pailleterie.

Georges (1843) is one of very few works by the author to touch upon his ancestry. Following the life of the eponymous Georges – the mixed race son of a plantation owner in the French colony of Mauritius – the novel addresses themes such as colonialism, racism, slavery and interracial intimacy.

When Dumas died on 5 December 1870, at the age of 68, he left behind a legacy of more than 100,000 published pages. His remains were initially kept in the family tomb built in Villers-Cotterêts for his father, who commanded Napoleon's cavalry in Egypt and Italy, but in 2002 during a celebration of the bicentury of the birth of both Hugo and Dumas, he was moved to the Panthéon.

During the lavish reburial ceremony, Dumas' coffin was escorted to the Senate in Paris by the mounted Garde Républicaine, before being carried to the Panthéon by four musketeers dressed in costumes designed by Jean-Charles de Castelbajac. No author since Victor Hugo has been transported to their final resting place in such style (though it has been disputed that Dumas would have preferred to remain buried in Villers-Cotterêts, as per his memoirs).

Château de Monte Cristo

Le Port-Marly, 78560
+33 (0) 1 39 16 49 49
Chateau-monte-cristo.com

Traveller's tip: To get to the château from Paris, take the Saint Nom la

Dumas' Château de Monte Cristo was completed in 1847 and the author threw a huge party to celebrate. I, JPGO

Dumas did most of his writing in the smaller Château d'If, which is also located on the grounds. Patrick Charpiat

Bretèche train from Paris Saint Lazare station to Marly le Roi station. Catch the number 10 bus towards "Les lampes" (avenue de l'Europe), getting off at Avenue Kennedy. Take the first turn on the right (Chemin des Montferrand) and follow the footpath to the Château de Monte Cristo.

While a trip to Château de Monte Cristo will take you out of Paris, it is still certainly worth a visit if you have a day to spare. Located on Port-Marly hill, between Marly-le-Roi and Saint-Germain-en-Laye, Dumas bought the plot of land at the height of his fame and hired Hippolyte Durand, a notable architect of the day, to create his perfect writing retreat.

The designs included a renaissance château standing in a garden filled with grottos, ornamental rocks and waterfalls, as well as a gothic castle in miniature, complete with its own moat, which Dumas named Château d'If. The hefty project was completed in 1847 with Dumas hosting a grand opening party for friends and admirers to mark the occasion.

Though he lived in the main building, it was in Château d'If that Dumas retreated for hours on end to write in peace and solitude, and the hideaway's facades are decorated with titles of his works and sculptures of his fictional heroes.

Perhaps unsurprisingly, given the extravagance of the designs, Dumas eventually went bankrupt and was forced to sell his beloved home in 1849. He was able to remain at Château de Monte Cristo with the consent of the buyer until 1851, when the author fled to Belgium to escape both his creditors and the wrath of Napoleon Bonaparte (who disapproved of the author).

Now a museum dedicated to the author, Château de Monte Cristo offers visitors the chance to explore Dumas' former house and gardens while learning about his works and larger-than-life personality.

Did you know? Along with Victor Hugo, Charles Baudelaire, Gérard de Nerval, Eugène Delacroix and Honoré de Balzac, Dumas was a member of the Club des Hashischins, which met monthly to take hashish at Hôtel de Lauzun (at that time Hôtel Pimodan) on the Île Saint-Louis in Paris.

3

WRITERS OF LA BELLE ÉPOQUE

La Belle Époque – or the beautiful era – is a term associated with the pre-war decades (roughly 1880–1914) that became defined by progress, prosperity, a flourishing of the arts and an exuberant *joie de vivre*.

Though rose-tinted by nostalgia (it was during the First World War that La

The Eiffel Tower was constructed between 1887 and 1889 following designs by Gustave Eiffel. Believed to be in Public Domain From Library of Congress, Prints and Photographs Collections

Belle Époque retrospectively received its romantic name), the idyllic view of the period has some basis in truth and, to this day, many believe it remains the City of Light's finest hours.

It was during this time that absinthe drinkers filled the bars of Pigalle, trendy cafés were packed with the movers and shakers of the bourgeoisie, artists such as Renoir, Monet and Picasso were hard at work painting scenes across the French capital, and writers flocked to Paris in their hordes.

The city itself was changing by the day: expansion of the railways, installation of the metro, and mass-production of bicycles then cars made travel and communications swifter and simpler, while electrification lit up the streets and cutting-edge fashion and design made Paris the international capital of style – not to mention the construction of the world-famous Eiffel Tower, which was built on the Champ de Mars for the Exposition Universelle of 1889.

In literary terms, both technological advances in printing and the Republic's relaxation of censorship laws led to a publishing boom. These are the years of Parisian Émile Zola's immense popularity as a novelist, of Colette's celebrity (and scandal) and of Guy de Maupassant's mastery of the short story.

La Belle Époque saw the installation of the Paris metro. © Chris Peilow

A thoroughly defining era, La Belle Époque has long since ended – crushed by the outbreak of the First World War – but its presence can still be seen and felt throughout Paris and, most especially, in the literary works created during this glitteringly optimistic period.

Émile Zola

The most famous writer of his day, Émile Zola (1840–1902) was born in Paris and subsequently raised by his mother in Aix-en-Provence, before returning to the city in 1858.

Although Zola completed his schooling at the Lycée Saint-Louis in Paris, he twice failed the *baccalauréat* exam, which was a prerequisite to further studies, and spent most of his early years unemployed and living in abject poverty. He subsisted by pawning his few belongings and, according to legend, by eating sparrows trapped outside his attic window.

Thankfully, he eventually found work as a mailing clerk for the publisher Hachette and in 1865 published his first novel, *La Confession de Claude* (1865; *Claude's Confession*). A sordid, semi-autobiographical tale that drew the attention of the public and police for its scandalous content, it also displeased his employer and so Zola quit his job to pursue his literary interests full-time.

The writer went on to pen *Thérèse Raquin* (1867) and *Les Rougon-Macquart (1871–1893)*, the latter a collective title given to a cycle of 20 novels which follow the lives of two branches of a fictional family living during the Second French Empire.

Renowned for his naturalist style – marked by its detached observations of life without idealism or avoidance of the ugly – in many of his novels Zola describes in intimate detail the day-to-day lives of ordinary Parisians, most especially the lowlier classes of French society.

Did you know? Zola won the Nobel Prize in Literature in 1901 and 1902.

Le Bon Marché

24 Rue de Sèvres, 75007
+33 (0)1 44 39 80 00
24s.com/fr-fr/le-bon-marche
Metro: Sevres – Babylone

"It was like a riot of colour, a joy of the street bursting out here, in this wide open shopping corner where everyone could go and feast their eyes."

Emile Zola, *Au Bonheur Des Dames*, 1883

A searing social commentary on the birth of consumer culture and capitalism, Zola's *Au Bonheur des Dames* (1883; *The Ladies' Delight*)

Le Bon Marché was one of the first modern department stores in the world. Guillaume Speurt

follows department store owner Octave Mouret, a shrewd manipulative man who exploits women and finds himself overcome with desire when a provincial girl arrives to work as his assistant.

According to author and critic Elaine Showalter, while researching *Au Bonheur des Dames* Zola spent five or six hours a day perusing Parisian shops for ideas and inspiration, but he was particularly fascinated with Le Bon Marché.

The now world-famous department store was the first of its kind, and today it is still as thriving as when it first opened in 1838. Housing a number of jewellery, fashion, homeware and perfume outlets, as well as an exhibition space, it is the perfect place to soak up the hustle and bustle of Paris' thriving shopping quarter.

Interior escalators at the iconic Bon Marché store. Jumilla

21 Rue de Bruxelles

Metro: Place de Clichy

Zola died unexpectedly and in rather curious circumstances on 29 September 1902. The victim of coal gas asphyxiation caused by a blocked chimney flue, his death was officially determined to be a tragic accident but there were – and still are – those who believe that the chimney may have been purposefully blocked by fanatical anti-Dreyfusards.

The conspiracy theory came about due to the scathing open letter written by Zola and published in 1898 on the front page of the Paris newspaper, *L'Aurore*, in response to the ongoing Dreyfus Affair. In the article, headlined *J'accuse*, Zola publicly denounced the highest levels of the French Army, accusing them of obstruction of justice and anti-semitism for wrongfully convicting Alfred Dreyfus to life imprisonment for allegedly communicating French military secrets to the German Embassy in Paris (Dreyfus was eventually exonerated in 1906 and reinstated as a Major in the French Army).

Plaque beneath Émile Zola's former apartment at 21 Rue de Bruxelles. © Chris Peilow

No foul play surrounding Zola's death has ever been proven and a plaque outside No. 21 Rue de Bruxelles commemorates the writer's life and works. While Zola's gravestone resides in Cimetière de Montmartre, his remains are now interred in the Panthéon alongside Hugo and Dumas.

Marcel Proust

Often regarded as one of the greatest authors of all time, Marcel Proust (1871–1922) created much of his work isolated from the world in a cork-lined room that he believed absorbed dust and pollen, and therefore didn't aggravate his asthma.

His *pièce de résistance* – the seven-part novel, *À la Recherche du Temps Perdu (1913-1927; In Search of Lost Time)* – is the story of Proust's own life told as an allegorical search for truth. The plot follows the narrator (who is never definitively named) as he comes of age, and explores the loss of innocence through experience, the vanity of human endeavour, and the triumph of sin and despair, though the narrator eventually concludes that all the beauty he has experienced is eternally alive and he sets to work, racing against death, to write the very novel the reader has just experienced.

Unlike many French authors Proust was greatly influenced by English writers, including Charles Dickens and George Eliot, and his prose still remains some of the most original and unique in all literature.

Proust's Bedroom

Musée Carnavalet, 23 Rue de Sévigné, 75003
+33 (0)1 44 59 58 58
carnavalet.paris.fr
Metro: Saint-Paul, Chemin Vert

According to his housekeeper, Celeste Albaret, Proust wanted no distractions

Plaque beneath Marcel Proust's former apartment at 102 Boulevard Haussman. © Chris Peilow

A plaque at 102 Boulevard Haussmann marks the building in which Proust lived and worked from 1907 to 1919, but at the Musée Carnavalet (the oldest museum in the City of Paris) visitors can view a replica of the room, complete with Proust's actual furniture.

The rest of the museum is worth exploring too. Covering the history of Paris from 4600bc to the twentieth century, it exhibits a number of remarkable paintings, sculptures and curios, including a gold watch-chronometer that belonged to Émile Zola.

Did you know? Proust is buried in Père Lachaise Cemetery, where it has become tradition for fans to place madeleines on top of his tomb (in a nod to *À la Recherche du Temps Perdu*, where a madeleine awakens the childhood memories of the narrator).

Sidonie-Gabrielle Colette

A boundary smashing figure who made her own rules, Sidonie-Gabrielle Colette (1873-1954) scandalised society with her liberated manner and fashion sense, enjoyed relationships with both genders, married three times and started a near-riot at the Moulin Rouge.

Generally known as Colette, the author was born in rural Burgundy and fell for Henry Gauthier-Villars, a music critic and writer, when she was barely out of her teens. A notorious libertine, Willy (Gauthier-Villars'

whatsoever from his work, and his writing implements were always arranged close at hand on a series of occasional tables in his room.

The room itself was simply decorated, containing just a single green-shaded lamp which provided the only source of light (the curtains remained tightly drawn) and the narrow bed which Proust had slept in since childhood.

And so, with Willy's encouragement, Colette continued to write a series of loosely autobiographical and sexually titillating novels which followed the coming-of-age and young adulthood of their titular heroine, Claudine.

Within three years Colette had written three more novels, and by 1903 when *Claudine s'en va* (*Claudine and Annie*) was published they were so popular that stores were selling everything from Claudine face powders to branded cigarettes, soaps, school hats, perfumes and dolls.

Despite the immense success of her work, Colette did not gain full credit for the novels until many years later as they were initially published under Willy's name. In fact, Willy exercised so much control over Colette's early literary career he kept the copyright of the novels for himself, while there is much speculation over the extent to which he forced his wife to write (there are rumours he locked Colette away in her study for up to four hours, or until she had finished her quota of pages for the day).

In a 1956 edition of *Claudine at School*, Colette penned her own introduction and said of the affair: "Being honorable, and above all indifferent, I kept silent about the truth, which did not become known until much later. Nevertheless, it is today for the first time that the Claudine books appear under the single name of their single author."

French author Sidonie-Gabrielle Colette.
Public Domain

nom-de-plume) took his new wife to Paris and introduced her to the avant-garde intellectual and artistic circles, and it was in the capital that he encouraged her to join the writing game.

Though Willy originally dismissed Colette's writings about a school girl called Claudine as useless, after leaving her work to languish in a drawer he stumbled upon them years later and realised what a blunder he had made. Lightly edited by Willy, *Claudine à l'école* (1900; *Claudine in School*) took Paris by storm and sold forty thousand copies in four weeks.

Eventually Willy and Colette's marriage came to an end and they separated in 1906 before divorcing four years later in 1910.

Though Colette had initially been a reluctant author (she fancied herself more of a dancer or actor), free from her husband Colette continued to write and it is perhaps her later works *Cheri* (1920) and *Gigi* (1944) which became her most enduring.

Did you know? Colette was nominated for the Nobel Prize in Literature in 1948.

Moulin Rouge

82 Boulevard de Clichy, 75018
+33 (0)1 53 09 82 82
Moulinrouge.fr
Metro: Blanche

While Colette was famed for her literary talents, it was her personal life which was often the talk of the bars and salons across Paris.

During a performance of the pantomime, *Rêve d'Égypte*, at the Moulin Rouge in 1907, Colette shared an onstage kiss with her lover Mathilde de Morny – who was playing a male Egyptologist in the show. Such a display of same-sex affection sparked so virulent a reaction from the audience that the production was immediately stopped, protests erupted and the police were called.

Sadly, the original Moulin Rouge – which was founded by Charles Zidler and Joseph Oller in 1889 – burned down in 1915, but it has since been rebuilt. The birthplace of the modern

The French cancan gained international fame at the Moulin Rouge cabaret. Nasreddine Nas'h

form of the cancan dance, the theatre still hosts dinners, dances and parties, and has become a very popular tourist destination.

9 Rue de Beaujolais

Metro: Pyramides or Bourse

Colette lived at this address between 1927 and 1929, and again from 1938 until her death in 1954. If you visit the building and look up, you will see a plaque on the first floor where Colette was often seen seated by the window as she wrote.

Travellers tip: A short walk from Rue de Beaujolais and just in front of the French institute, Comédie-Française, lies Place Colette. The square received its name in 1966 as a tribute to the author at the request of her only daughter, Colette de Jouvenel.

Guy de Maupassant

A prolific writer and disciple of fellow author Gustave Flaubert (1821–1880), Guy de Maupassant (1850–1893) established the grand heights of his literary talents with the immense success of his short story *Boule de Suif* (1880; *Ball of Fat*).

Continuing to write fervently for the next decade, Maupassant became

Plaque beneath Colette's apartment at 9 Rue de Beaujolais. © Chris Peilow

one of the most prolific authors of his time, producing an estimated 300 short stories, 200 newspaper articles, 6 novels and 3 travel books

In his later years the author became ravaged with syphilis, which greatly affected his mental health, causing him to suffer paranoid delusions which cut short his writing career.

Boulevard des Italians

Metro: Opéra, Richelieu-Drouot

Many of Maupassant's characters inhabit a world of material desires where lust, greed and ambition are the sole driving forces, and none more so than in *Bel-Ami* (1885; *Dear Friend*). Inspired by the author's observations of the slick businessmen and cynical journalists living and working in Paris, *Bel-Ami* is a scathing satire on a societal class who let nothing stand in the way of their scramble to the top.

During Maupassant's time, the Boulevard des Italians was a regular stamping ground for the city's bourgeoisie, surrounded as it was by the stock exchange, theatreland, glut of newspaper offices and trendy cafés. It is along this grand boulevard that the drama of *Bel-Ami* unfolds, as the reader follows protagonist George Duroy's journey from a down-and-out ex-soldier to the ruthless, womanising chief editor at newspaper, *La Vie Français*.

Echoes of the Boulevard des Italians as seen in Maupassant's novel are still present today. Home to numerous cafés and shops, the bustling boulevard is a good place to stop for a bite to eat and a taste of busy Parisian life.

Hotel Intercontinental – Café de la Paix

5 Place de l'Opéra, 75009
+33 (0)1 40 07 36 36
Cafédelapaix.fr/en
Metro: Opéra

It didn't take long after its opening in 1862 for this majestic hotel to become the toast of Paris' literary elite, attracting the likes of Hugo, Zola (who had the heroine of his book, *Nana*, die on the hotel's third floor), Proust, Maupassant and Oscar Wilde.

This bundle of famous writers enjoyed many nights eating, drinking and holding court in the hotel's legendarily lavish Café de la Paix, which remains open to this day.

Designed in the Napoleon III style by architect Alfred Armand, the interior rivals that of the Opéra Garnier itself (think magnificent chandeliers, baroque ceilings and fluted columns) and was declared a *monument historique* by the French government in 1975.

Renovated in 2002 by the Bâtiments de France – a state-run architectural firm specialising in historic preservation – Café de la Paix still retains much of its charm and remains a Parisian institution, with a culinary repertoire that includes traditional

The famous Café de la Paix is located on the northwest corner of the intersection of the Boulevard des Capucines and the Place de l'Opéra. © Chris Peilow

staples such as steak tartare, French onion soup and foie gras. There is also a chic terrace which offers unrivaled views of the Opéra Garnier.

Montparnasse Cemetery

3 Boulevard Edgard Quinet, 75014
Metro: Edgar Quinet, Raspail

Although Maupassant appeared outwardly healthy and athletic, with the passing of the years he became increasingly sombre, due in part to an advancing case of syphilis. On 2 January 1892 the author tried to end his life and was committed to a private asylum in Paris, before dying one month before his 43rd birthday on 6 July 1893.

Today you can visit Maupassant's grave in the peaceful Montparnasse Cemetery. Covering 19 hectares, the cemetery offers a haven of quiet and calm at the heart of one of the liveliest districts in Paris and is home to more than 35,000 graves, making it the second largest necropolis in the city (after Père Lachaise Cemetery).

Wellwishers often place pens on Guy de Maupassant's grave at Montparnasse Cemetery in tribute to the writer. Public Domain

4

WILDE ABOUT PARIS

Dublin-born Oscar Wilde. Public Domain

Though Oscar Wilde (1854–1900) is a prolific figure of La Belle Époque, his life varied quite dramatically from that of his Parisian contemporaries. For a start he was born in Dublin, Ireland, before moving to London in the early 1880s, where his biting wit and panache proved popular amongst artistic and social circles.

Wilde's first foray into the City of Light didn't occur until the summer of 1874. He was 19 at the time and holidaying with his mother, and the pair checked into the Hotel du Quai Voltaire (which still stands today and is within a stone's throw of Le Louvre and Tuileries Gardens).

The writer immediately fell in love with the bustling bistros, lively salons and overall decadence of Paris, so much so he would return on many occasions to hobnob with his fellow literary elites, wine and dine extravagantly, and make a name for himself amongst the upper echelons of French society (where he impressed with his fluent grasp of the language).

However, Wilde's Paris is a tale of two cities: the exuberant, bright city of literary and social acclaim before his imprisonment, and the place to which he would eventually return after his dramatic fall from grace.

Did you know? One person who was not so taken by Wilde's verbosity was Victor Hugo, who supposedly fell asleep while meeting the writer.

Le Grand Café Capucines

4 Boulevard des Capucines, 75009
+33 (0)1 43 12 19 00
legrandcafe.com
Metro: Opéra

Wilde's regular stamping ground during his Parisian sojourns was the Left Bank, around Saint-Germain-des-Prés, where he engaged in animated discussions with the likes of André Gide, Stéphane Mallarmé and Paul Verlaine.

On occasion the author also ventured across to the Right Bank, where he partook in Paris' fine dining offerings before attending the opera.

Given his lavish tastes, Café de la Paix became a favourite haunt of the author's, as well as the Parisian gem that is Le Grand Café Capucines. Open until midnight everyday, the brasserie serves traditional French cuisine to the highest standards (their fresh seafood is legendary).

Théâtre de l'Athénée

7 Rue Boudreau, 75009
+33 (0)1 53 05 19 19
athenee-theatre.com
Metro: Opéra

In 1891 Wilde rented lodgings on the Boulevard des Capucines (near to his favourite local, of course), and it was while staying here that he penned the one-act tragedy, *Salomé.*

A retelling of the attempted seduction of John the Baptist by Salomé, the step-daughter of Herod Antipas, and his eventual execution at Salomé's instigation, the play was banned in the UK for its depiction of biblical events on stage (which was forbidden at the time). However, the same rules did not apply in France and *Salomé* was published in 1893 by the *Librairie de L'Art Independent.*

Le Grand Café Capucines offers seafood platters, oysters and lobster in an opulent 1800s setting. © Chris Peilow

The Théâtre de l'Athénée is classified as a historical monument and still runs nightly performances.
© Chris Peilow

Three years later, in 1896, the play made its stage debut at the Théâtre de la Comédie-Parisienne. Sadly, by the time of the play's opening Wilde was serving a prison sentence for illegal homosexual activity and so never managed to see the performance.

Théâtre de la Comédie-Parisienne has since been renamed Théâtre de l'Athénée, and the intimate, Italian-style establishment still hosts a number of avant-garde performances, as well as revivals of operetta and musical comedy. For the latest listings and tickets make sure to check their website.

L'Hôtel

13 Rue des Beaux Arts, 75006
+33 (0) 1 44 41 99 00
l-hotel.com
Metro: Saint-Germain-des-Prés

At the height of his success Wilde enjoyed enormous fame and popularity. His novel *The Picture of Dorian Gray* (1891), as well as his plays, *A Woman of No Importance* (1893) and *The Importance of Being Earnest* (1895), filled book shops and theatres across London's West End, but in 1895 his life took a catastrophic turn for the worst.

Guests can stay in the bedroom at L'Hôtel where Oscar Wilde spent his final moments. Courtesy of l'Hôtel

> **OSCAR WILDE**
> Poéte et Dramaturge
> NÉ À DUBLIN
> LE 15 OCTOBRE 1856
> EST MORT DANS CETTE MAISON
> LE 30 NOVEMBRE 1900

Plaque outside L'Hôtel commemorating Wilde's death. Courtesy of l'Hôtel

During the nineteenth century homosexuality was illegal in the UK, and on 25 May 1895 Wilde was charged with gross indecency for his sexual relations with men. After a much publicised trial the jury found him guilty and Wilde was sentenced to two years hard labour, which he served at Newgate Prison, then Pentonville Prison, and finally at Reading Gaol (which inspired his poem, *The Ballad of Reading Gaol*).

On his release in 1897, Wilde immediately left the UK never to return. He went first to Dieppe, France, and then, in 1898, settled in Paris. Over the next two years the former socialite cut a desperate, destitute figure stretching out the hours by smoking and drinking in his usual haunts, which he paid

Views from a room balcony at L'Hôtel. Courtesy of l'Hôtel

for by borrowing money from passing friends and acquaintances.

Wilde's last address was at the Hôtel d'Alsace, where he passed away on 30 November 1900 from cerebral meningitis, aged 46. Despite his failing health, Wilde's wit stayed with him until the very end. In reference to the wallpaper adorning his hotel room, his last words are rumoured to have been: "My wallpaper and I are fighting a duel to the death. One of us has got to go."

The wallpaper won, but guests can still request the Oscar Wilde Suite –

that is, the room where he died – at the renamed L'Hôtel. Far from being a macabre or garish experience, the five star suite is tastefully decorated and drenched in a luxurious style Wilde himself would have appreciated, complete with green and gold wallpaper, a vintage writing desk and a large private terrace.

The room also features a collection of fascinating Wildeiana, including a copy of a letter from the hotel manager at the time which implores Wilde – or Sebastian Melmoth, as he called himself then – to pay for his stay.

Being unable to locate the funds, Wilde famously commented: "I am dying above my means."

Traveller's tip: L'Hôtel also has a fantastic bar called Oscar's lounge, named after their famous former client.

Père Lachaise Cemetery

Boulevard de Ménilmontant, 75020
pere-lachaise.com
Metro: Philippe Auguste

Immediately after his death Wilde was buried in a leased pauper's grave in Bagneux, just outside the walls of Paris. However, in 1909, when Wilde's bankruptcy was paid off by the posthumous sales of his works, his longtime friend and alleged former lover, Robert Ross, moved his remains to Père Lachaise Cemetery – the most prestigious necropolis in Paris.

Wilde's tomb was designed by Sir Jacob Epstein and took ten months to complete. The epitaph inscribed into the stone is a verse from Wilde's poem, *The Ballad of Reading Gaol*:

And alien tears will fill for him
  Pity's long-broken urn,
For his mourners will be outcast men,
  And outcasts always mourn.

Today, Wilde's tomb remains one of the most visited plots in the entire cemetery, attracting thousands of

Wilde's grave in Père Lachaise Cemetery.
© Chris Peilow

wellwishers each year. In the nineties a tradition developed whereby visitors would apply lipstick and then kiss the tomb. However, the cleaning operations to remove the lipstick grease caused the stone to become more porous, damaging Epstein's work, and so in 2011 the Irish government paid to install a glass barrier around the bottom half of the monument. Many Wilde fans remain unfettered and now kiss the glass barrier instead.

Situated in the 20th arrondissement, Père Lachaise Cemetery covers 44 hectares and contains 70,000 burial

Père Lachaise Cemetery is the most visited necropolis in the world. © Chris Peilow

plots, so it can be a little hard to navigate but it is certainly worth a visit. Tours run daily (apart from Fridays), or if you wish to explore the leafy walkways and gothic burial chambers alone, the Porte du Repos pedestrian entrance features a handy map to help locate the most interesting and elaborate tombs.

Did you know? As far as cemeteries go, Père Lachaise takes some beating. Wilde shares his final resting place with the likes of Moliere, Frédéric Chopin, Eugène Delacroix, Honoré de Balzac, Colette, Jim Morrison, Gertrude Stein, Richard Wright and Marcel Proust, as well as the fictional Jean Valjean from *Les Misérables.*

Balzac's grave in Père Lachaise Cemetery.
© Chris Peilow

5

THE LOST GENERATION LITERATI

Though France was rocked by the horrors of the First World War, by the early 1920s the *Années Folles* (crazy years) of Paris were in full swing. The City of Light became the creative capital of the western world with locals, expats and tourists embracing all the extravagance and hedonistic decadence Paris had to offer (which was a lot).

The bars filled up once more, parties went on until the early hours and the salons were flooded with budding

Les Deux Magots become a regular hang-out for the Lost Generation. © Julio Piatti

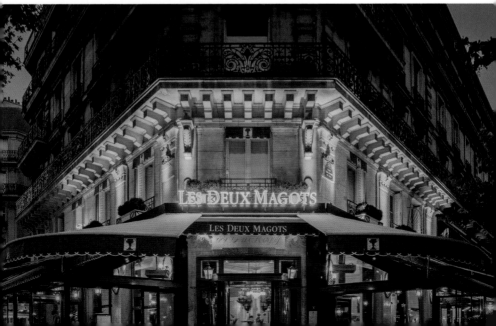

writers hoping to make their mark on the literary world.

Americans were particularly attracted to Paris. Disenchanted by President Warren G. Harding's post-war "return to normalcy" campaign, they found the bohemian lifestyle offered by the French much more appealing.

Writers emigrated across the pond in their dozens, often spending their days scribbling novels in the cafés lining the Left Bank and their nights frequenting lavish parties to drink to excess. Thus, the Lost Generation was born.

Despite such debauchery, the *Années Folles* would eventually become known as the golden age of literary modernism, and the writers of this time produced some of the most famous works in history, including F. Scott Fitzgerald's *The Great Gatsby* (1925) and Ernest Hemingway's *The Sun Also Rises* (1926).

Did you know? According to Hemingway's *A Moveable Feast* (1964), the term 'Lost Generation' was originally coined by art collector and writer Gertrude Stein, who overheard a garage owner in France refer to the younger generation as a "*génération perdue.*" Stein agreed, feeling that the war had caused them to lose their way and so, in utter disillusionment, they'd turned to heavy-drinking and fast-living.

Lovers often place padlocks along the River Seine bridges. © Chris Peilow

Gertrude Stein's salons

27 Rue de Fleurus, 75006
Metro: Saint-Placide, Rennes

"It was easy to get into the habit of stopping in at 27 Rue de Fleurus for warmth and the great pictures and the conversation"
Ernest Hemingway,
A Moveable Feast, 1964

27 Rue des Fleurus, the location of Stein's salons.
© Chris Peilow

Born in Allegheny, Pennsylvania, Gertrude Stein (1874–1946) settled in Paris in 1903 and her apartment on 27 Rue de Fleurus became famous for its salons, which brought together confluences of talent and thinking that would help define modernism in literature and art as we know it.

Though Stein attributed the beginnings of her salons to artist Henri Matisse, it is well-known that she possessed a unique and seemingly unequalled ability to detect talent in others. Soon she had not only amassed an impressive art collection – the paintings of Delacroix, Renoir and Gaugin adorned her apartment walls – but the likes of Pablo Picasso, Paul Cezanne, F. Scott Fitzgerald, Ezra Pound and Ernest Hemingway made her Saturday evening salons an important and regular fixture in their diaries.

During these salons the writers and artists would gather to discuss anything and everything, from their latest works, to goings-on in Paris and America, as well as asking Stein for feedback on their art and writing (her judgments were so

Author and art collector Gertrude Stein. Public Domain

revered it is thought she could make or break careers with her chance remarks).

Although Stein's apartment is not open to the public, a plaque at 27 Rue de Fleurus marks the address of the historic salons, while fans of Stein can visit Père Lachaise Cemetery where she shares a grave with her lifelong partner, Alice B. Toklas.

Did you know? Fellow American Natalie Clifford Barney also hosted a weekly literary salon at 20 Rue Jacob, where guests would meet to discuss art, drink, dance and read Sappho's poetry.

Hemingway's haunts

"Such was the Paris of our youth, the days when we were very poor and very happy."
Ernest Hemingway, *A Moveable Feast*, 1964

Ernest Hemingway, Paris, circa 1924. Public Domain - Ernest Hemingway Photograph Collection, John Fitzgerald Kennedy Library, Boston.

Ernest Hemingway (1899–1961) and Paris go together like fresh croissants and coffee. Though he was American by birth – as well as enjoying travels throughout Spain, Cuba and Africa – nowhere is as heavily associated with the author than the French capital.

It was in Paris that Hemingway began writing novels, and where he penned his lauded debut, *The Sun Also Rises*. Thanks to Hemingway's richly detailed memoir, *A Moveable Feast* (published posthumously), fans of the writer can retrace his exact footsteps through the city he loved so much, from the places he wrote to the places he wrote about.

Did you know? Hemingway was awarded the Nobel Prize in Literature in 1954 for his novel, *The Old Man and the Sea* (1952).

74 Rue du Cardinal Lemoine
Metro: Cardinal Lemoine

Hemingway volunteered as an ambulance driver during the war and was seriously injured while serving on the Italian front in 1918. Four years later he moved to Paris with his first wife, Hadley Richardson, and the young couple rented an apartment on Rue du Cardinal Lemoine in the 5th arrondissement.

Far from playing host to the beautiful bistros and trendy restaurants that line

Place de la Contrescape is filled with bustling French bistros and eateries, making it the perfect place to stop for lunch. © Chris Peilow

A plaque marking the location of Hemingway's flat at 74 Rue du Cardinal Lemoine on the Left Bank.
© Chris Peilow

the Latin Quarter today, in Hemingway's time the area was a working-class neighbourhood full of down-and-out artists and writers. In fact, the apartment Hemingway rented had no running water or indoor toilet facilities.

Hemingway initially came to Paris as a journalist working for the *Toronto Star*, but he was determined to become an author. To this end he took another room in a hotel around the corner at 39 Rue

Descartes, where he could concentrate on his writing without distraction.

Recounting how he spent his time writing alone, Hemingway wrote in his memoir:

"I brought mandarines and roasted chestnuts to the room in paper packages and peeled and ate the small tangerine-like oranges and threw their skins and spat their seeds in the fire when I ate them and roasted chestnuts

Rue Mouffetard runs down the hill to the church of Saint Médard and is one of the best market streets in Paris. Hemingway recalls it fondly in his memoir, and today you'll still find numerous food stalls filled with fruit and vegetables lining the pavements, as well as grocers offering authentic French charcuterie, cheeses and pastries, and a smattering of coffee shops and bars.

Traveller's tip: Many stalls close from lunchtime onwards, so get there early to soak up the atmosphere.

Les Deux Magots

6 Place Saint-Germain-des-Prés, 75006
+33 (0)1 45 48 55 25
lesdeuxmagots.fr/en
Metro: Saint-Germain-des-Prés

when I was hungry. I was always hungry with the walking and the cold and the working."

Though neither buildings are open to the public, there are commemorative plaques on the walls outside each apartment.

Traveller's tip: The nearby Place de la Contrescarpe is a lively square with many café terraces to enjoy a spot of lunch and people-watching.

Marché Mouffetard

Rue Mouffetard, 75005
Metro: Censier-Daubenton

Notoriously headstrong with a penchant for drink (the author particularly enjoyed a scotch and soda or a dry martini), Hemingway spent much of his waking hours enjoying the vibrant bars, cafés and restaurants Paris had to offer. One of his regular stops was Les Deux Magots, which was also frequented over the years by James Joyce, Albert Camus, Simone de Beauvoir and Jean-Paul Sartre.

Today the bistro's reputation precedes itself. Not only has the Deux Magots literary prize been awarded to a French novel every year since 1933, but the bistro has been

Les Deux Magots is now a popular tourist destination. © Julio Piatti

mentioned in Vladimir Nabokov's *Lolita* (1955), Katherine Neville's *The Magic Circle* (1998), China Miéville's *The Last Days of Paris* (2016), and Steve Matchett's *The Chariot Makers* (2004), where he describes Les Deux Magots as, "the first café in the quarter to be blessed by the morning sun. Its clientele pay a healthy premium for drinking there, it's only fitting they should be the first to catch the warmth of the new day."

Did you know? The name, Les Deux Magots, originates from the two Chinese figurines that still adorn the bistro's interior.

Brasserie Lipp

151 Boulevard Saint-Germain, 75006
+33 (0) 1 45 48 53 91
brasserielipp.fr/en
Metro: Saint-Germain-des-Prés

This charming brasserie in the 6th arrondissement was amongst Hemingway's favourite lunch spots. In *A Moveable Feast* the author fondly recounts sitting at one of the small tables to enjoy a litre of beer (*un distingué*). Though the brasserie no longer serves beer by the litre, it remains much the same as it was in the 1920s, with Hemingway's preferred dish (*pommes a l'huile*) still on the menu.

Hemingway could often be found lunching at Brasserie Lipp. © Chris Peilow

Did you know? Brasserie Lipp sponsors the Prix Cazes, an annual award given to an author who has won no other literary prize.

Harry's New York Bar

5 Rue Daunou, 75002
+33 (0) 1 42 61 71 14
harrysbar.fr/language/en
Metro: Opéra

Tucked away down a small street in the 2nd arrondissement, Harry's New York Bar holds numerous claims to fame.

Not only was it one of the many bars Hemingway frequented of an evening, but fellow Lost Generation writer F. Scott Fitzgerald was also a regular, while George Gershwin composed his hit musical *An American in Paris* in the downstairs piano bar and British writer Ian Fleming is thought to have been fond of the joint; in *A View To Kill* (1960), James Bond calls Harry's New York Bar the best place in Paris to get "a solid drink".

In fact, Harry's New York Bar was such a staple on the hard-drinking

The cocktails at Harry's New York Bar enjoy a stellar reputation. © Chris Peilow

Sank Roo Doe Noo sign outside Harry's New York Bar. © Chris Peilow

circuit that it ran advertisements in the international press which told English-speaking visitors arriving in Paris to simply ask taxi drivers for "Sank Roo Doe Noo" – an anglicised play on the bar's address, 5 Rue Daunou.

Did you know? The bar also claims to have created classic cocktails such as the Side Car and French 75.

Bar Hemingway

15 Place Vendôme, 75001
+33 (0)1 43 16 33 74
ritzparis.com
Metro: Opéra, Madeleine

"When I dream of an afterlife in heaven, the action always takes place in the Paris Ritz"
Ernest Hemingway.

Nestled inside the Hôtel Ritz, legend has it Hemingway celebrated France's victory over the Germans by drinking 51 dry martinis in a row while seated in this bar.

Renamed after its most famous patron, Bar Hemingway is awash with quirky memorabilia – look out for old typewriters, Hemingway's handwritten letters and a framed pack of his Lucky Strike cigarettes – while the tufted

The legendary Bar Hemingway inside the Ritz, Paris. © Vincent Leroux

leather armchairs, sepia photographs and richly wood-panelled walls will make you feel as if you've slipped back in time.

Did you know? The Ritz was also a favourite of Fitzgerald's and is mentioned in his works *Babylon Revisited* (1931) and *Tender is the Night* (1934).

Traveller's tip: The pocket-sized bar has just 25 seats and the cocktails – which are printed on a newspaper and

Left: *Bar Hemingway – cocktail.* © Bernhard Winkelmann

Below: *Entrance to Hôtel Ritz.* © Chris Peilow

Opposite: *Inside the Suite Impériale at Hôtel Ritz.* © Vincent Leroux

include twists on the classics, such as a Lemon Charlie and the Ritz Pimms – cost upwards of €30.

When Hemingway met Fitzgerald

"The American in Paris is the best American. It is more fun for an intelligent person to live in an intelligent country. France has the only two things toward which we drift as we grow older – intelligence and good manners"

F. Scott Fitzgerald

Paris was as much a playground for F. Scott Fitzgerald (1896–1940) as it was for Hemingway. Unlike his fellow expats,

Fitzgerald's more refined tastes meant he often preferred the elegant bistros and glitzy salons of Paris' Right Bank to the unabashed bohemia of the Rive Gauche.

Born in Saint Paul, Minnesota, Fitzgerald attended Princeton University – though he dropped out before graduating – and in 1920 his first published novel, *This Side of Paradise*, cemented his reputation as one of the eminent writers of the decade.

The work was a triumph and was regarded as a revelation of the new morality in the early Jazz Age. It brought Fitzgerald almost immediate financial success and fame, and the young writer suddenly found himself mingling with high society and experiencing all the benefits that came with it. It was thanks to his newfound status that his muse, Zelda Sayre, who came from a prominent Southern family, finally agreed to marry him.

By the time the Fitzgeralds moved to Paris in 1925 the Roaring Twenties were in full swing. The couple took up residence on 14 Rue de Tilsitt in the 8th arrondissement, just a stone's throw from the Champs-Elysées, and in true Gatsby style Fitzgerald threw himself into the thick of the debauchery, enjoying all the glitzy parties and excessive drinking that Paris had to offer. On numerous occasions the couple would spend the evening quaffing champagne and cocktails at the Hôtel Ritz or dancing at Ada "Bricktop" Smith's cabaret, before losing the early hours in the trendy bars of Montmartre and Pigalle.

Of course, it wasn't all fun and games. Fitzgerald dedicated his days to writing, as well as getting to know his fellow American expats, and none more so than Hemingway.

Did you know? Fitzgerald dubbed his wife, Zelda, "the first American flapper" and her bobbed hair, fashion sense, and unapologetic drinking and dancing epitomised the Roaring Twenties.

La Closerie des Lilas

171 Boulevard du Montparnasse, 75006
+33 (0)1 40 51 34 50
closeriedeslilas.fr/en
Metro: Vavin

Though Fitzgerald and Hemingway's initial meeting occurred in The Dingo Bar (now an Italian restaurant called L'Auberge de Venise) according to *A Moveable Feast* it was seated at La Closerie des Lilas that Hemingway first read *The Great Gatsby* at Fitzgerald's request.

Similar to Les Deux Magots, La Closerie des Lilas was a regular watering hole for the great artistic and literary minds of Paris, and from this rendezvous the two authors struck up a fast friendship bonding over their love of literature and drinking, which they indulged in together and often.

Though their relationship deteriorated over the years into a tense and complicated rivalry, they continued to write to one another and critique each other's work. In one instance, in 1934, Fitzgerald asked Hemingway for feedback on his newly released novel, *Tender is the Night*. Hemingway did not hold back, giving Fitzgerald a scathing critique on the characters, plot and honesty of the writing.

Sadly, the two great writers met tragically early ends. As the Roaring Twenties fizzled to an end, Fitzgerald sobered to the reality of his crumbling marriage and began drinking more and more heavily. In 1930, when his wife, Zelda, was diagnosed with schizophrenia, the Fitzgeralds left Paris for good to return to America.

Once a favourite of Fitzgerald and Hemingway, La Closerie des Lilas still serves fine wines and French delicacies in a picturesque setting. DIMSFIKAS

Interior of La Closerie des Lilas. Celette

After a long struggle with alcoholism, Fitzgerald attained sobriety only to die of a heart attack in 1940, aged 44.

When Hemingway heard of Fitzgerald's death he was living in Cuba with his third wife and, despite their former friendship, he did not attend Fitzgerald's funeral.

In 1959 Hemingway moved to Idaho where he tried to continue writing but, anxiety-ridden and depressed, in 1961 he committed suicide.

While there is no denying Hemingway and Fitzgerald battled many demons, Les Closarie des Lilas still stands as a reminder of the two great writers during the prime of their lives. Today, the iconic restaurant offers typical French brasserie fare and has retained the ambiance of old world Paris thanks to its red leather booths, mahogany bar and live music, while the leafy terrace is perfect for dining al fresco in the warmer months.

Did you know? Now considered one of the greatest books ever written, *The Great Gatsby* did not become a success until after Fitzgerald's death.

THE HARLEM RENAISSANCE

"It's a great city, Paris, a beautiful city"
James Baldwin, *Another Country*, 1962

The Harlem Renaissance saw a boom in the revival of African American culture, and while the epicentre of this spectacularly influential movement was Harlem, New York City, many key figures found themselves fleeing the racial discrimination of the United States to pursue their lives and art more freely in Europe.

A burgeoning African American community had existed in Paris since the First World War, when 350,000 black Americans were brought over to France, the vast majority of which came from the American South. Rather than return to the discriminatory Jim Crow laws which awaited them back in America, when the fighting was over many of these soldiers decided to stay in France, where they found themselves able to enjoy their lives more freely.

In the coming years hundreds of black musicians, dancers and entertainers, such as Josephine

Baker, Ada "Bricktop" Smith and Louis Armstrong, ventured across the pond to join them, while novelists Richard Wright (1908-1960), Claude McKay (1889-1948), James Baldwin (1924-1987) and Chester Himes (1909-1984) also helped pioneer a more permanent African American literary and artistic community in Paris.

Caveau de la Huchette is an iconic jazz club in the Latin Quarter. © Caveau de la Huchette

Caveau de la Huchette. © Caveau de la Huchette

Traveller's tip: Caveau de la Huchette is a must for any jazz fans. Musician Sidney Bechet was once a regular performer at the club, which plays live music and is open from 9pm until 2am every night.

Montmartre

Metro: Abbesses, Blanche Station, Anvers

It was during the Harlem Renaissance that jazz was first introduced to the French, and in Montmartre the black community found a welcome home in jazz clubs Le Grand Duc, Chez Florence and Bricktop's. These clubs burst to life every evening, and the sounds of saxophones and trumpets rang through the streets of Montmarte for almost two decades, until the occupation of the city by German troops on 18 June 1940 caused many artists to flee or go undercover.

Though the jazz clubs have long since closed their doors, Montmarte remains one of Paris' most charming areas and a popular tourist spot. By day the district is filled with street artists playing music or painting caricatures, eclectic art galleries and romantic

The Sacré-Cœur in Montmartre. © Chris Peilow

The Montmartre Funicular runs daily. © Chris Peilow

terraces for lunch and drinks – and there's even a little train which offers daily tours. As night falls, the area comes alive with its abundance of busy bars and restaurants – not to mention the fantastic views across Paris from the steps in front of the Sacré-Coeur Basilica.

If you're interested in the history of Montmartre, then a visit to the local museum (Musée de Montmartre, 12 Rue Cortot) offers fascinating insights into bohemian life in the village during the nineteenth and twentieth century.

Traveller's tip: Why not swap the stairs for a ride on the funicular? Located right at the foot of Montmartre hill, beneath the Sacré-Coeur Basilica, the funicular opened in 1900 (though it has been rebuilt since) and will take you to the top of the famous Rue Foyatier steps in 90 seconds.

14 Rue Monsieur le Prince

Metro: Odéon

Author Richard Wright was born on a plantation in Mississippi and visited Paris with his family in 1946, before settling in the capital in 1947. His work focused on race, sex and politics, and by 1948 the success of his novel *Native Son* (1940) and the memoir *Black Boy* (1945) had amassed him enough money to buy the large apartment that still stands at 14 Rue Monsieur le Prince in the Latin Quarter.

His neighbour, Sylvia Beach, became a close friend and it was Wright who

Plaque outside Richard Wright's former residence on Rue Monsieur le Prince. © Chris Peilow

encouraged her to write her memoirs, which would later be named after her publishing company, Shakespeare & Company. Beach also spoke highly of her new acquaintance, even writing to her sister to say:

"Of all the writers I have known, he is the most unselfish and thoughtful... Fellas like Hemingway appear uncouth beside Dick Wright."

Wright eventually became a French citizen and went on to publish seven books between 1953 and 1958, including the semi-autobiographical *The Long Dream* (1958). Today, there is a plaque outside the building commemorating the importance of Wright's work, which made a lasting impact on race relations in the United States and Europe.

Le Select

99 Boulevard du Montparnasse, 75006
+33 (0)1 45 48 38 24
leselectmontparnasse.fr/en
Metro: Vavin

In the mid-1950s when Chester Himes moved to Paris, he was already an established writer in the United States after the critical acclaim of his novels, *If He Hollers Let Him Go* (1945) and *Cast the First Stone* (1952).

As an expatriate in the French capital, Himes could often be found working on his novels in the heated terrace at Le Select in Montparnasse. Focusing his talents on a series of black detective novels set in New York's Harlem, the first novel of the series, *A Rage in Harlem* (1957), is filled with swagger, dark humour and lurid violence, and won Himes the Grand Prix de Littérature Policière.

Fellow author James Baldwin was also a regular patron at Le Select, and today the café continues to serve up top-notch coffee and a particularly delicious Rum Baba.

Le Select on the Left Bank is still as bustling now as it was after the war. Celette

Café Tournon

18 Rue de Tournon, 75006
+33 (0)1 43 26 16 16
letournon.fr
Metro: Odéon

Nestled just north of Jardin du Luxembourg, Café Tournon became a regular port of call for African American writers such as James Baldwin, Richard Wright and William Gardner Smith. According to Hazel Rowley's biography, *Richard Wright: The Life and Times* (2001), Wright often stopped by here in the afternoons to enjoy a coffee and play the pinball machine. In fact, rumour has it Wright spent so much time at the café (which was round the corner from his apartment) that the locals started referring to it as "Dick's place".

Did you know? Journalist George Plimpton became a regular at Café Tournon in the 1950s, and it was here that literary magazine *The Paris Review* first took shape under Plimpton's leadership.

7

POST-WAR PARIS

Just as the Second World War left a lasting mark on the world, so too did the literary scene change irrevocably. In the aftermath of the German occupation many writers were still drawn to Paris, but the exuberance and hedonism enjoyed by the Lost Generation during the inter-war years was no longer *en vogue*.

This was a period charged with conflicting emotions and politics, of intellectual change and debate, and while the spirit of newfound freedom was intense, the trauma of what had come before played heavily on the minds of Parisians.

For the huge number of foreigners travelling to Paris, rediscovering the most elegant city in the world was a true indulgence after so many years at war. And while Paris was still calibrating and rebuilding, the theatres, cabarets, bistros, haute couture shops and hotels were soon

The Arc de Triomphe honours those who fought and died for France in the French Revolutionary and Napoleonic Wars. © Chris Peilow

filled with their much-missed clientele of diplomats, philosophers, artists and writers.

Due to the large concentration of bookstores and publishing houses situated in Saint-Germain-des-Prés, many writers rented small rooms or apartments in the area. Similar to their Lost Generation predecessors, to escape their meagre lodgings they took full advantage of the fashionable cafés lining the Left Bank, and the literary scene bounced back with a vengeance.

Philosopher, playwright and novelist Jean-Paul Sartre (1905–1980) rose to huge prominence during this period. Joined by his lifelong partner, Simone de Beauvoir (1902–1986), Sartre frequented the many cafés of the Left Bank to eat, write and discuss his views on existentialism. The intense and illuminating conversations between these two incredible minds continue to inspire books, films and schools of thought to this day.

It was also during this time that Françoise Sagan (1935–2004) found almost overnight fame for her debut novel *Bonjour Tristesse* (1954; *Hello Sadness*), while the Beat Generation arrived in Paris to experiment with new forms of poetry and prose, bringing with them their own flavour of sexual liberation and vivacious energy.

Rue de Buci has always been a hub of creative activity. © Chris Peilow

The Beats in Paris

In the 1950s Paris became the temporary playground of the Beat Generation. William S. Burroughs (1914–1997), Allen Ginsberg (1926–1997) and Jack Kerouac (1922–1969) were the core founders of the group after meeting at New York's Columbia University in 1944, where they first began exploring themes and subjects which focused on sexual liberation, spiritual quests, experimentation with psychedelic drugs and the rejection of materialism, while

Relais Hôtel du Vieux Paris – plaque. © Chris Peilow

The Beat Hotel (Relais Hôtel du Vieux Paris) on the Left Bank. © Chris Peilow

their work also prominently featured intense portrayals of the human condition.

Though the movement was centred mainly in the bohemian artist communities of San Francisco's North Beach, Los Angeles' Venice West and New York City's Greenwich Village, between 1957 and 1963 the most important centre of activity for the Beat Generation was Paris, and most especially Relais Hôtel du Vieux Paris.

Relais Hôtel du Vieux Paris

9 Rue Gît-le-Cœur, 75006
+33 (0) 1 44 32 15 90
vieuxparis.com/en
Metro: Saint-Michel Notre-Dame

"This fleabag shrine will be documented by art historians"
Harold Norse,
Beat Hotel, 1975

When Ginsberg, Kerouac and Burroughs arrived in Paris in the late 1950s they took up residence at a rundown hotel at 9 Rue Gît-le-Coeur on the Left Bank. Though nameless at the time, thanks to its newly acquired inhabitants the poet Gregory Corso christened the establishment the Beat Hotel and the name stuck.

Nestled among the rat run of streets in the Latin Quarter, the hotel had just 42 rooms and was a class 13 establishment – the lowest possible standard of hotel. The rooms had windows facing the interior stairwell and were poorly lit, hot water was only available on Thursdays, Fridays and Saturdays, and each landing had a Turkish *chiotte* (a traditional, hole-in-the-floor toilet).

Thankfully there was an opportunity to bathe – in the only bathtub, located on the ground floor – provided guests reserved a time beforehand and paid an extra fee (though sometimes the owner of the hotel, Madame Rachou, accepted poems and drawings in lieu of money).

It was inside this legendary hotel that Brion Gysin introduced Burroughs to the 'cut-up' literary technique, in which pre-existing texts, taken initially from newspapers and magazines, were cut-up and juxtaposed to form new phrases. Using this technique Burroughs wrote his celebrated masterpiece, *Naked Lunch* (1959), which was first published in Paris and is now considered among the key works of twentieth century US literature.

While the hotel has since changed hands and been transformed into the four-star establishment that is Relais Hôtel du Vieux Paris, it's still worth stopping by to view framed photographs of Burroughs, Ginsberg and Corso in the lobby, as well as a plaque outside which commemorates its former status as the Beat Hotel.

Did you know? Because of US obscenity laws, a complete American edition of Burroughs' *Naked Lunch* wasn't published until 1962.

Jean-Paul Sartre and Simone de Beauvoir

Born and bred Parisians, Beauvoir and Sartre met in 1929 while studying the agrégation in philosophy – a highly competitive postgraduate examination. Aged 21, Beauvoir was the youngest person to have ever sat the exam and ended up coming second in class to Sartre's first.

Jean-Paul Sartre and Simone de Beauvoir together in 1955. Public Domain

and were allowed to pursue other sexual partners. In Beauvoir's own words: "We were two of a kind, and our relationship would endure as long as we did: but it could not make up entirely for the fleeting riches to be had from encounters with different people."

Did you know? One of the most influential thinkers of the twentieth century, the impact of Sartre's work was recognised in 1964 when he was awarded the Nobel Prize in Literature. The author, however, refused this coveted accolade, the first person ever to do so, declaring "a writer should not allow himself to be turned into an institution."

This initial meeting spawned what would become one of the most legendary relationships in recent French history. For 51 years, until their deaths in the 1980s, Beauvoir and Sartre were almost inseparable, enjoying a romantic relationship while also working side-by-side as writers and philosophers. They became the leaders of existentialism - a philosophy that rejected all absolutes and talked of freedom, personal choice and authenticity - and lived out their gloriously modern union at various cafés, hotels and jazz clubs across Paris, though they never married

Sorbonne Université

21 Rue de l'Ecole de Médecine, 75006
+ 33 (0) 1 40 46 23 39
sorbonne-universite.fr
Metro: Cluny La Sorbonne

The Sorbonne Université – also known as the University of Paris – has been considered one of the most prestigious centres of intelligence, culture, science and arts in the world since the thirteenth century.

A functioning university to this day, it is where Sartre and Beauvoir studied together. Guests can visit the historic institution and its grounds with tours running from Monday to Friday, as well as one Saturday each month.

Entrance to Sorbonne University. Mbzt

Did you know? The Sorbonne's notable alumni also includes writers Balzac, Hugo, Françoise Sagan and T.S. Eliot, as well as Marie Curie and Pope Benedict XVI.

La Coupole

102 Boulevard du Montparnasse, 75014
+ 33 (0)1 43 20 14 20
lacoupole-paris.com/en
Métro: Vavin, Montparnasse Bienvenüe

Sartre and Beauvoir were regulars at the increasingly popular Les Deux Magots and Café de Flore on the Left Bank (visitors are still able to sit at Sartre's exact corner table). Far from losing their days to alcoholic excess like their Lost Generation predecessors, the couple sat silently at separate tables to focus on their own work or to edit that of the other – Sartre often commented that Beauvoir "filtered" his words.

As the couple's notoriety grew and Les Deux Magots and Café de Flore became too crowded, the pair would decant to the nearby La Coupole in the Montparnasse district. Opened in 1927, La Coupole is listed as a historical monument and the brasserie's 33 pillars, decorated by the painter Alexandre Auffray, and superb floor mosaic deserve a visit on their own.

Did you know? La Coupole's famous lamb curry has remained on the menu since 1927 and is a firm customer favourite.

Hôtel La Louisiane

60 Rue de Seine, 75006
+33 (0) 1 44 32 17 17
hotel-lalouisiane.com
Metro: Mabillon

Between 1943 and 1948 Beauvoir stayed at Hôtel la Louisiane. Reportedly, it is while here that she had the epiphany which would lead to her foundational feminist work, *Le Deuxième Sexe* (1949; *The Second Sex*).

The book made a seismic impact on feminist thinking, going into great detail examining and dismantling

Café de Flore is one of the oldest coffee houses in Paris and has welcomed the likes of Sartre, Beauvoir, Hemingway and Fitzgerald. © Chris Peilow

certain patriarchal myths that Beauvoir said constrained women into becoming the lesser, or second, sex.

Following its publication, Beauvoir became somewhat of a figurehead for the next surge of women's rights activism in France. She continued to champion women's causes for the rest of her life, giving financial backing to many feminist groups, defending women in the Algerian war and campaigning for the legalisation of abortion in France.

In fact, Beauvoir made such a name for herself as a feminist thinker that when she died in 1986 the newspaper announcing her death ran with the headline: "Women, you owe her everything!"

Hôtel la Louisiane is still open to visitors and has a long history of welcoming artists and writers like Beauvoir, including Salvador Dali, Albert Camus and Henry Miller, as well as director Quentin Tarantino and The Rolling Stones.

If you fancy an overnight stay then rooms are basic but clean, and prices are very reasonable. It might also help to know Beauvoir stayed in room 68, while Sartre took the famously round room 10.

Did you know? If you're interested in Hôtel la Louisiane, director Michel La Veaux released a documentary about the hotel's colourful history in 2015.

Place Jean-Paul-Sartre-et-Simone-de-Beauvoir
Metro: Saint-Germain-des-Prés

One of the few squares in Paris named after a couple (others include

Place Jean-Paul-Sartre-et-Simone-de-Beauvoir. Connie Ma

Lousie-Catherine-Brelau-et-Madeleine-Zillhardt and allée Claude-Cahun-Marcel-Moore), for nearly two decades after the war Sartre and Beauvoir lived close by at 42 Rue Bonaparte.

While at this address Sartre published some of his best-known works, including *La Mort dans L'âme* (1949; *Troubled Sleep*) and his autobiography *Les Mots* (1964; *The Words*). He continued writing for the rest of his life and in 1980 passed away from an edema of the lung. On the day of his funeral, more than 50,000 Parisians descended on Boulevard du Montparnasse to accompany his cortège as it passed by his favourite haunts on the way to his final resting place at Montparnasse Cemetery

After Sartre's death, Beauvoir gave a moving account of his later years in *La Cérémonie des Adieux* (1981; *Adieux, A Farewell to Sartre*). Six years later Beauvoir died from pneumonia, and she now rests side-by-side with her lifelong partner.

Françoise Sagan

The most popular literary event of 1954 came in the form of 18-year-old Françoise Sagan's debut novella, *Bonjour Tristesse*. Unlike the *nouveaux romanciers* which were increasingly *en vogue* at the time, Sagan's story of adolescent love was

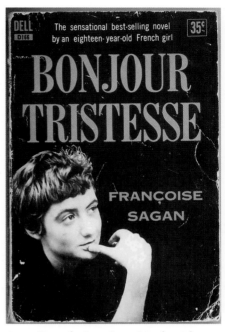

Cover of Françoise Sagan's novel, **Bonjour Tristesse.**
Christo Drummkopf

written with more 'classical' restraint and brought instant celebrity and notoriety to the teenager, who would go on to have a long and colourful career.

Before her rise to literary fame, Sagan was born Françoise Quoirez in the Lot valley to bourgeois parents, who also kept an apartment in Paris' prosperous 17th arrondissement. Expelled from two schools in her younger years, Sagan wrote her debut while attending a crammer to prepare for a retake of her baccalaureate. Not much studying was done – although she managed to pass the exam to enrol at the Sorbonne – and instead Sagan spent several hours a day seated in a Parisian café writing in her blue exercise book.

Within three months her manuscript was complete, and just days after delivering her work to the offices of publisher René Julliard, on Rue de l'Université, a telegram was delivered to Sagan at her parent's apartment on Boulevard Malesherbes asking her to contact them immediately.

Bonjour Tristesse was published not long after. The novella became an overnight success, while also causing a stir among French society with its scandalous portrayal of a sexually liberated 17-year-old woman and her roué father.

Such an accomplished debut marked the start of the author's prolific literary career. Sagan went on to live a riotous life, filled with fast cars, scandal and drama, and though she wrote dozens more plays and novels – including *Un Certain Sourire* (1956; *A Certain Smile*) which follows a Sorbonne student's affair with a middle-aged man – none of her later works quite matched the heights of *Bonjour Tristesse*.

Did you know? Sagan wrote her own obituary for the *Dictionary of Authors*, which read:

"Appeared in 1954 with a slender novel, *Bonjour Tristesse*, which created a scandal worldwide. Her death, after a life and a body of work that were equally pleasant and botched, was a scandal only for herself."

167 Boulevard Malesherbes
Metro: Malesherbes, Wagram

On 12 February 2020 the City of Paris unveiled a commemorative plaque at Sagan's previous home on Boulevard Malesherbes to honour the author and her fervent love of the capital.

Interestingly, author Alexandre Dumas also lived on Boulevard Malesherbes in the 1860s at number 107.

Did you know? The pseudonym 'Sagan' was taken from a character in Marcel Proust's *À la Recherche du Temps Perdu*.

Plaque outside Françoise Sagan's former residence at 167 Boulevard Malesherbes. © Chris Peilow

8

WRITERS OF TODAY

Still drawn to the magnetic pull of the City of Light, writers from the world over continue to use Paris as their muse, either by traversing the broad boulevards on their own two feet or allowing their characters to do the exploring for them.

If you're heading to Paris (or already there) then you're going to need a reading list worthy of such a magical place. Though not an exhaustive collection, below are some of the latest and greatest novels set in the city during the last century, along with some scenic spots to enjoy them in.

Paris remains filled with aspiring writers and enthusiastic readers © Chris Peilow

River Seine. © Chris Peilow

All the Light We Cannot See by Anthony Doerr (2014)

Written by American author Anthony Doerr, *All the Light We Cannot See* won the Pulitzer Prize for Fiction in 2015 as well as the 2015 Andrew Carnegie Medal for Excellence in Fiction.

Opening in Paris in 1934 the story follows Marie-Laure LeBlanc, who has been blind since the age of six and has learned to traverse the labyrinthine city sightless with the help of her father, Daniel. When the Nazis invade Paris the pair flee to St Malo, a walled city by the sea, where Marie-Laure is drawn ever closer to Werner, a German orphan who was destined to labour in the mines until a broken radio brought him to the notice of the Hitler Youth.

A deeply moving novel, Paris is vividly brought to life through the sounds and smells encountered by the young LeBlanc, and the descriptions of the Jardin des Plantes in the 5th arrondissement are particularly evocative. Located in the grounds of Paris' Natural History Museum, the botanical garden offers plenty of benches to sit and read peacefully, as well as walkways to enjoy a stroll through the fauna.

The Jardin des Plantes is the main botanical garden in France. Benh Lieu Song

Jardin des Plantes

57 Rue Cuvier, 75005
+33 (0) 1 40 79 56 01
jardinsdesplantesdeparis.fr
Metro: Jussieu, Quai de La Rapée

Paris For One by Jojo Moyes (2015)

While Jojo Moyes' bestselling novel, *Me Before You,* closes on the banks of the Seine, in this delightful story Moyes chooses to set her entire story in Paris. The tale follows Nell, a meticulous and organised 26-year-old who has never left home, but when she arranges a visit to Paris with her boyfriend and he doesn't show up, she is forced to explore the city alone.

Having never done so much as eat in a restaurant by herself, Nell embarks on a journey of self-discovery as she makes new friends, enemies and acquaintances, including an American businesswoman and a handsome French waiter.

A charming short story, *Paris for One* is brimming with romance and the underrated pleasures of solo travel.

The Da Vinci Code by Dan Brown (2003)

It's impossible to write a travel guide about books and Paris without mentioning Dan Brown's worldwide bestseller, *The Da Vinci Code.* Following symbologist Robert Langdon and cryptologist Sophie Neveu, the novel begins with a murder at the Louvre Museum, which sends the pair on a journey to discover whether Jesus

The Louvre Pyramid at night. Benh Lieu Song

Christ and Mary Magdalene bore a secret child together.

Brown's book has gone on to sell more than 80 million copies worldwide, and was made into a feature film in 2006 starring Tom Hanks.

Musée du Louvre

Rue de Rivoli, 75001
+33 (0)1 40 20 53 17
louvre.fr/en
Metro: Palais-Royal – Musée du Louvre, Louvre – Rivoli

Traveller's tip: The Louvre Museum is huge – approximately 38,000 objects are exhibited over an area of 72,735 square metres – and impossible to cover in one day, so make sure to plan out which pieces you'd like to see

in advance (and expect queues for Leonardo da Vinci's Mona Lisa).

Paris Echo by **Sebastian Faulks (2018)**

Many novels set in Paris tend to romanticise the city (and rightly so), but this novel shows Paris as a harsh and unforgiving place, filled with the lonely and the lost.

Faulks' tale follows two strangers, Tariq, a Moroccan teenage runaway, and Hannah, an American academic, who arrive in the City of Light for very different reasons. Though the pair have little in common, they are both trapped by the ghosts of the past, with Hannah studying the wartime experiences of women living there under German occupation, and Tariq searching for information about a dead mother he barely knew.

The Little Paris Bookshop by **Nina George (2003)**

This heart-warming international bestseller is a love letter to books and Paris. Set on a beautifully restored barge on the Seine, bookseller Jean Perdu runs what he likes to call a literary apothecary, for he possesses a rare gift for sensing which books will soothe the troubled souls of his customers.

The only person he is unable to cure is himself. He has nursed a broken heart ever since the love of his life fled Paris, leaving behind a handwritten letter that he has never dared read. His memories and his love have been gathering dust, until the arrival of an enigmatic new neighbour in his eccentric apartment building on Rue Montagnard. When Perdu is tempted into reading the letter, he immediately sets off on a mission to make peace with his loss and discover the end of his own story.

Murder on the Eiffel Tower by Claude Izner (2007)

Painstakingly researched and beautifully written, *Murder on the Eiffel Tower* can easily be devoured in one sitting. Set in late-nineteenth-century Paris, a young woman dies in the brand new Eiffel Tower – but can a bee sting really be the cause of death? Young bookseller Victor Legris doesn't believe so, and is determined to find out what really happened.

As the first novel in the best-selling series of murder mysteries starring Legris, *Murder on the Eiffel Tower* won the prestigious Michel Lebrun French Thriller Prize in 2003. If you enjoy this instalment, then try *The Père-Lachaise Mystery* (2003) and *The Montmartre Investigation* (2003), both also set in Paris and penned by Izner (a pseudonym for authors Liliane Korb and Laurence Lefèvre, who write the novels together).

The Eiffel Tower

Champ de Mars, 5 Avenue Anatole, 75007
toureiffel.paris
+33 (0)8 92 70 12 39
Metro: Champ de Mars-Tour Eiffel

A view of Place du Trocadéro from the top of the Eiffel Tower. © Chris Peilow

Traveller's tip: For great views and photographs of the Eiffel Tower, head across Pont d'Iéna to Place du Trocadéro.

A Night at the Majestic by Richard Davenport-Hines (2006)

Based on a real event, *A Night at the Majestic* opens one May night in 1922 at the Majestic Hotel (now called Hotel Raphaël) when five of the greatest artists of the twentieth century sat down to supper.

This would be the only time Joyce, Proust, Picasso, Diaghilev and Stravinsky were in a room together. Summoned by British art connoisseur and playboy Sydney Schiff to celebrate the premiere of Stravinsky's burlesque ballet *Le Renard*, Schiff's ulterior motive was to bring together these five great icons of modernism for one historic meeting.

A celebration of Parisian high-life and filled with lively anecdotes and sharp observations, it's a truly delightful read.

Hotel Raphaël

17 avenue Kléber, 75116
+33 (0)1 53 64 32 00
raphael-hotel.com
Metro: Kléber

Traveller's tip: Hotel Raphaël's rooftop is open to the public and offers 360° panoramic vistas across Paris, including unbeatable views of the Eiffel Tower, Arc de Triomphe and Sacré Cœur.

The Hôtel Raphaël (formerly Hôtel Majestic) remains emblematic of Parisian glamour in the Roaring Twenties. © The Peninsula Paris

The Elegance of the Hedgehog by Muriel Barbery (2006)

Set in modern day Paris, unlikely heroine Renée works as a concierge in a grand Parisian apartment building at 7 Rue de Grenelle – one of the most elegant streets in Paris.

An autodidact in literature and philosophy, Renée hides this rare skill to avoid the condemnation of the building's tenants. Meanwhile, several floors up, 12-year-old Paloma Josse is determined to avoid the pampered and vacuous future laid out for her by her parents, and decides to end her life on her next birthday. But unknown to both Renée and Paloma, the sudden death of one of their privileged neighbours will alter the course of their lives forever.

Selling more than 6 million copies worldwide, Le Figaro named it "the publishing phenomenon of the decade".

The Piano Shop on the Left Bank by T.E. Carhart (2000)

One for music lovers, The Piano Shop on the Left Bank tells the autobiographical tale of an American living in Paris who yearns to return to piano playing after many years absence. Intertwined with a story of friendship are reflections on how pianos work, their fascinating history, and tales of the people who create and care for them.

The Paris Wife by Paula McLain (2011)

A female counterpart to Hemingway's A Moveable Feast, McLain's novel is told from the point of view of the author's wife, Hadley Richardson, and provides a fictional account of their life which is often at odds with that shown in his own work.

The novel opens with a 28-year-old Richardson meeting Hemingway for the first time and falling for his energy, intensity and burning ambition to write As in real life, they marry after a brief courtship and move to Paris, which is in full swing of the Jazz Age and filled with artists and writers fuelling their nights with alcohol, partying and gossip. But is such a place conducive to a happy and healthy marriage? As their relationship begins to flounder, the birth of their beloved son serves only to drive the couple further apart.

Time Was Soft There: A Paris Sojourn at Shakespeare & Co. by Jeremy Mercer (2006)

Jeremy Mercer's memoir recounts the anecdotes, curiosities and personalities he encountered during the five months he spent living inside the Shakespeare & Company bookstore in 2000. Run by an eccentric octogenarian named George Whitman, the iconic bookstore across the river from the Notre-Dame Cathedral is still open today and has become a refuge for writers, misfits and lost souls everywhere.

Aspiring writers who sleep among the novels at Shakespeare & Company are affectionately referred to as Tumbleweed. © Chris Peilow

Did you know? Writers and artists can sleep free of charge inside Shakespeare & Company. In return, they are asked to read a book a day, help out in the shop for a couple of hours and write a single-page autobiography for Whitman's archives.

9

BOOKSHOPS AND BIBLIOTÈQUES

Paris is a soup pot of book browsing opportunities. In fact, you're almost never further than a stone's throw away from a lively bouquiniste or sleepy bibliothèque, so here are some of the best for hunting down your next read.

Book browsing. © Chris Peilow

Shakespeare & Company

37 Rue de la Bûcherie, 75005
+33 (0) 1 43 25 40 93
shakespeareandcompany.com
Metro: Saint-Michel Notre-Dame

"I created this bookstore like a man would write a novel, building each room like a chapter, and I like people to open the door the way they open a book, a book that leads into a magic world in their imaginations"

George Whitman

Shakespeare & Company has a fascinating history and has become one of the most celebrated bookshops in the world. Started by American expat Sylvia Beach in 1919, it was originally located at 12 Rue de l'Odéon and allowed customers to buy or borrow books, while also serving as a functioning publishing house.

Soon Beach's charming establishment became a home away from home for many expats, who would while away the hours chatting to Beach or perusing the dozens of books on offer. Writers from Aimé Césaire to Beauvoir,

The famous exterior of Shakespeare & Company bookshop. © Chris Peilow

Shakespeare & Company entrance door. © Chris Peilow

Shakespeare & Company – Shakespeare.
© Chris Peilow

James Joyce, Hemingway and Stein became members – and would have been chased up for late returns with Beach's drawing of an exasperated Shakespeare pulling out his hair.

The bookstore remained open until the Germans occupied Paris in 1941. One day that December a Nazi officer entered the store and demanded Beach's last copy of *Finnegans Wake,* which he'd seen displayed in the window. Beach refused, and the officer threatened to return to confiscate all of her goods and shut down the bookstore. With the help of her friends, Beach packed up the thousands of books and files, photographs and furniture in a matter of hours and moved everything to a vacant flat in the same building.

A year later, Beach was arrested and interned for six months at a camp in Vittel. After her release she went into hiding in a students' hostel at 93 Boulevard Saint-Michel and her bookshop would never reopen.

Thankfully a second location (the one you can visit today) was started in 1951 by American George Whitman. Initially named Le Mistral, Whitman changed it to Shakespeare & Company in April 1964 in honour of Beach and her incredible bookstore.

Still nestled on the banks of the Seine, Whitman's bookshop remains a meeting place for anglophone writers and readers the world over, as well as a reading library and a purveyor of new and second-hand books. Inside you'll find a labyrinth of passages, alcoves and reading rooms with plenty of secret corners and cosy spots for curling up in with a good book.

An onsite café also opened in 2015 which sells coffees and cakes, while Beach fans can find a memorial plaque at the location of the original Shakespeare & Company at 12 Rue de l'Odéon.

Did you know? Beach's Shakespeare & Company became the first publisher to print James Joyce's classic, *Ulysses*, in 1922. At the time no other publishing houses dared due to its "obscene" content, which had seen it banned in the US and UK.

Traveller's tip: If you purchase a book from Shakespeare & Company you can have it inscribed with a special stamp, a tradition started by the shop in the 1950s.

The Bouquinistes of Paris

Bords de Seine, 75004
Metro: Saint-Michel Notre-Dame, Pont Marie (Cité des Arts)

Paris' bouquinistes have been standing for centuries and now carry UNESCO

The bouquinistes lining the Seine remain an integral part of Parisian culture. Ninara

World Heritage status. The dark green stalls dot the River Seine on both sides – from Pont Marie to Quai du Louvre on the Right Bank, and Quai de la Tournelle to Quai Voltaire on the Left Bank – amassing to more than 226 booksellers who sell anything a bookworm could need, from new and old literature, to vintage magazine covers, pocket fiction, graphic novels, antique maps, book marks and souvenirs.

Just as Hemingway and Fitzgerald once did, it's easy to lose a day riffling through the many treasures on offer – especially when they're open every day from morning until dusk.

La Librairie du Passage

48 Passage Jouffroy, 75009
+33 (0) 1 56 03 94 10
librairiepassages.fr
Metro: Grands Boulevards

Nestled in the charming Passage Jouffroy – also home to the Grévin Museum and a plethora of boutiques selling antique toys – La Librairie du Passage sells both new and old volumes, with a particular focus on visual arts, architecture and ancient tomes. With its vintage wooden panelling and a team of passionate staff, you're sure to find something of interest – even if it is only the fabulous interior.

La Librairie du Passage. © Chris Peilow

Librairie Galignani

224 Rue de Rivoli, 75001
+33 (0) 1 42 60 76 07
galignani.fr
Metro: Tuileries

When Giovanni Antonio Galignani opened his bookstore in Paris in 1801, it would become the first English bookshop established on the continent (a plaque outside the building marks this impressive accolade).

The original Librairie Galignani stood on Rue Vivienne, but it has since relocated to Rue de Rivoli and English readers should walk straight through to the back of the store (passing an incredible International Fine Arts section full of art books which would look fabulous on any coffee table), where they'll find a comprehensive selection of titles in English, with a strong emphasis on modern fiction and classics.

The store itself is still run by direct descendants of the original Galignani family, and the walls are so filled with books there are multiple library ladders dotted about to reach the higher shelves (although ask permission first).

Librairie Delamain

155 Rue Saint-Honoré, 75001
+33 (0) 1 42 61 48 78
librairie-delamain.com
Metro: Palais-Royal – Musée du Louvre

Librairie Galignani. © Chris Peilow

Librairie Delamain. Jacques Giral © Agence Lonsdale

Librairie Delamain interior. Jacques Giral © Agence Lonsdale

Founded in 1700 by the Delamain family in the Comédie-Française arcades, Librairie Delamain has since moved to 155 Rue Saint-Honoré. Jean Cocteau, Colette, Louis Aragon and François Mitterrand were all fans of this bookstore, and with its rustic wooden bookshelves, library ladders and exceptional collection of over 5,000 classics, it's not hard to see why.

Librairie Jousseaume

45–47 Galerie Vivienne, 75002
+33 (0)1 42 96 06 24
librairie-jousseaume.com
Metro: Palais-Royal – Musée du Louvre, Bourse

Hidden within one of the most beautiful arcades in Paris, Librairie Jousseaume is a veritable treasure trove. Now a listed building, Jousseaume opened its doors in 1826 and draws bibliophiles from across the globe. Filled with old books and all the charm of a bygone era, visiting this old-world bookstore almost feels like stepping back in time.

L'eau et Les Rêves bookstore

9 Quai de l'Oise, 75019
09 51 55 08 75
penichelibrairie.com
Metro: Ourcq, Crimée

Librairie Jousseaume. © Chris Peilow

L'eau et Les Rêves is a floating bookshop on a barge. © Chris Peilow

Interior of L'eau et Les Rêves. © Chris Peilow

Docked on Quai de l'Oise you'll find L'eau et Les Rêves. Aptly named (the title means 'water and dreams' in English), this bookshop on a barge stocks works mostly dedicated to travel, the sea and nature. With an onsite café and outdoor terrace, it's the perfect pit stop for a touch of caffeine and escapism.

La Belle Hortense

31 Rue Vieille du Temple, 75003
+33 (0)1 48 04 71 60
Metro: Hôtel de Ville

The pretty blue frontage marks the entrance to this little literary gem,

which is stocked full of books and bottles of wine, and hosts regular readings and events. An absolute must for all bibliophiles.

The Abbey Bookshop

29 Rue de la Parcheminerie, 75005
+33 (0) 1 46 33 16 24
abbeybookshop.org
Metro: Cluny La Sorbonne

An independent bookshop in the heart of Paris' Latin Quarter, The Abbey Bookshop is the sort of place bookworms dream about. The shop sits on the tranquil Rue de la Parcheminerie and the entrance is marked by a large

La Belle Hortense. © Chris Peilow

Above: *The Abbey Bookshop.* © Chris Peilow

Right: *Interior of The Abbey Bookshop.* © Chris Peilow

Canadian flag, in honour of the shop's founder, Brian Spence, who hails from Toronto.

Spence crossed the Atlantic to bring his bookstore to an international audience in 1989, and now The Abbey Bookshop offers more than 40,000 new and used titles – which line every inch of the walls and staircase – as well as free tea and coffee for anyone needing a brief respite from the hustle and bustle of the Rive Gauche.

San Francisco Books Company

17 Rue Monsieur le Prince, 75006
+33 (0)1 43 29 15 70
sfparis.com
Metro: Odéon

Specialising in second-hand books, the San Francisco Books Company is an ideal port of call for those searching for a good book on a tight budget. Thousands of volumes fill the shelves at the friendly shop, which first opened in 1997, and you'll find everything from history novels to books on art, science, philosophy and religion, as well as a great children's section, comic books and a collection of first editions.

The American Library in Paris

10 Rue du Général Camou, 75007
+33 (0) 1 53 59 12 60
americanlibraryinparis.org
Metro: École Militaire, Alma-Marceau

With such a rich history of American writers in Paris, it's only fitting for the city to house the largest English language lending library in Europe. Just a stone's throw from the Eiffel Tower, The American Library in Paris opened in 1920 with a collection of books donated by American libraries for the use of army personal serving in the city during the war.

Having expanded since then, today it stocks thousands of English books and also hosts free evening presentations by authors, scholars, journalists and other public figures, so be sure to check out their events calendar.

Traveller's tip: The American Library in Paris is a private lending library and, unless you're a member, there's a €10 day fee to enter.

San Francisco Books Company. © Jim Carroll, courtesy of the San Francisco Bookshop

Author Angie Thomas (right) speaking to young American Library members in early 2020. © Julien LB, courtesy of The American Library in Paris

Bibliothèque Mazarine

23 Quai de Conti, 75006
+33 (0)1 44 41 44 06
bibliotheque-mazarine.fr
Metro: Saint-Germain-des-Prés, Pont Neuf

Originally created by Cardinal Mazarin as his personal library in the seventeenth century, the Bibliothèque Mazarine contains one of the richest collections of rare books and manuscripts in France, and is the oldest public library in the country.

Located within the Palais de l'Institut de France, the library is also home to a Gutenberg Bible, which dates back to 1250 and is kept in a vault – though a facsimile copy is on display in the reading room.

Open to all, Bibliothèque Mazarine is worth a visit simply for its stunning façade and interior, while the library also organises free guided tours which are conducted by a curator at the end of the day and focus on the history of the library and its collections.

Bibliothèque Mazarine is located within the Palais de l'Institut de France. © Chris Peilow

Bibliothèque Mazarine. © Amy Murell

Bibliothèque Publique d'Information

Place Georges-Pompidou, 75004
+33 (0)1 44 78 12 75
bpi.fr/bpi
Metro: Rambuteau

Since its controversial opening in 1977 the Centre Georges Pompidou has attracted millions of visitors, yet few are familiar with the four-story media library located on the Rue Beaubourg side of the building.

An impressively modern library, Bibliothèque Publique d'Information is open daily – but if you're looking to get some work done be sure to arrive early as desks fill up quickly.

Bibliothèque Sainte Geneviève

10 Place du Panthéon, 75005
+33 (0)1 44 41 97 97
bsg.univ-paris3.fr
Metro: Cardinal Lemoine

Located opposite the Panthéon, the grand interior of the Bibliothèque Sainte Geneviève is just as impressive as the library's exterior, which is engraved with the names of great minds who made contributions to the body of human knowledge, including Galileo, Copernicus and Shakespeare.

Most days you're likely to find students from the University of Paris queuing alongside the building to get a seat in the immense reading room, but the library is open to all.

Exterior of the Centre Pompidou. © Chris Peilow

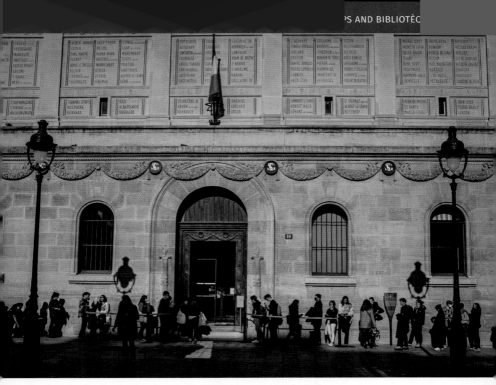

University of Paris students queuing outside Bibliothèque Sainte-Geneviève. © Chris Peilow

Did you know? Bibliothèque Sainte Geneviève appears as a setting in Honoré de Balzac's *Les Illusions Perdues*, James Joyce's *Ulysses* and the novels of Simone de Beauvoir.

Bibliothèque Marguerite Durand

79 Rue Nationale, 75013
+33 (0)1 53 82 76 77
Metro: Olympiades

Founded in 1932 by the eponymous journalist, actress and suffragette, this library holds a fascinating collection of historical items – including brochures, letters, photographs, periodicals and art pieces – and texts relating to feminism and women's history.

It remains the only French public library exclusively devoted to the history of women, feminism and, in recent years, gender studies.

Bibliothèque Richelieu

58 Rue de Richelieu, 75002
+33 (0)1 53 79 53 79
bnf.fr
Metro: Bourse, Quatre Septembre

The Oval room inside Bibliothèque Richelieu. Vincent Desjardins

Situated between the Palais Royal and Galeries Vivienne, the Bibliothèque Richelieu is one of the four branches of the Bibliothèque National de France (which was originally founded at the Louvre Palace in 1368 under Charles V).

The site houses some of humanity's earliest writings, as well as a collection of ancient Greek and Roman pottery and an immense Oval Room. It's open every day except Sundays, and the gardens offer a tranquil respite from the busy city.

Bibliothèque de l'Arsenal

1 Rue de Sully, 75004
+33 (0)1 53 79 39 39
bnf.fr
Metro: Sully-Morland

The Bibliothèque de l'Arsenal, located just a few steps from the Bastille, is another branch of the Bibliothèque National de France. One of the smaller libraries in Paris, it makes up for its size with plenty of history and charm.

The building dates back to the seventeenth century, though it wasn't

Entrance to Bibliothèque de l'Arsenal. © Chris Peilow

Cannon found on the grounds of Bibliothèque de l'Arsenal. © Chris Peilow

turned into a library until the French Revolution in 1797. Step inside to take a peek at the magnificent Salon de Musique and room of illustrations, or to browse the library's occult documents, including original manuscripts of *The Sacred Magic of Abra-Melin*, *Book of the Penitence of Adam* and the *Grimoire of Armadel*.

Bibliothèque Forney

1 Rue du Figuier, 75004
+33 (0)1 42 78 14 60
Metro: Pont Marie (Cité des Arts)

Easily one of the most secluded and beautiful libraries in Paris, Bibliothèque Forney sits on a quiet corner behind Pont Marie and specialises in decorative arts, including fashion and design. Inside you'll find 23,000 volumes of work, as well as 50,000 exhibition

Bibliothèque Forney – sign. © Chris Peilow

Bibliothèque Forney is a rare example of medieval civil architecture in Paris. © Chris Peilow

catalogues, 4,000 newspaper titles and a rich iconographic collection.

Tours are on offer, though if the times don't fit your schedule it is still worth a visit to admire the courtyard and beautifully restored spires, staircases and archways of the gorgeous gothic building.

Médiathèque Françoise Sagan

8 Rue Léon Schwartzenberg, 75010
+33 (0)1 53 24 69 70
mediathequeducarresaintlazare.
wordpress.com
Metro: Gare de l'Est

One of the largest libraries in Paris, Médiathèque Françoise Sagan is of course named after the celebrated author of *Bonjour Tristesse*. Opened in 2015 on the site of the Saint-Lazare hospital (which was used to house people with leprosy), it has an impressive collection of books, DVDs and vinyls, and is a must-see for anyone interested in film and media arts.

Traveller's tip: The surrounding Mediterranean courtyard and sprawling palm trees is a great spot for lunch al fresco.

Médiathèque Françoise Sagan. © Chris Peilow

Bibliothèque Historique de la Ville de Paris

24 Rue Pavée, 75004
+33(0)1 44 59 29 40
Metro: Saint-Paul

This public library specialises in the history of Paris, bringing together documents dating from the sixteenth century all the way to present day. Access is available to approximately one million books and booklets, plans, maps, photographs and 21,000 manuscripts which cover a variety of topics about the French capital. Heaven for history buffs.

Bibliothèque Historique de la Ville. © Chris Peilow

WHERE TO STAY

If you're going to follow in the footsteps of your favourite characters and authors, you might as well live like them too.

Hotel Le Swann

11–15 Rue de Constantinople, 75008
+33 (0) 1 45 22 80 80
hotel-leswann.com
Metro: Europe
Le Swann hotel is part of the Hôtel Littéraire society and is the first of

its kind entirely devoted to Marcel Proust. Set in the heart of the historically Proustian quarter of Plaine Monceau, Le Swann's 81 rooms are dedicated to characters in the author's *À la Recherche du Temps Perdu* as well as artists he admired, such as painter Giotto and author Anna Noailles.

Each floor is also named after fictional places in the Proust's

Hôtel Le Swann's 81 rooms are named after characters in Proust's À la Recherche du Temps Perdu *as well as famous artists the author admired.* © Hôtel Le Swann

masterpiece and guests have access to a library of 500 books written by or about the author, as well as photographs and paintings of the author – and there's even a themed cocktail menu.

Hotel Monte Cristo

20-22 Rue Pascal, 75005
+33 (0)1 40 09 09 09
hotelmontecristoparis.com/en
Metro: Les Gobelins, Censier-Daubenton

Every detail of the Hotel Monte Cristo draws its inspiration from the extraordinary personality of Alexandre Dumas. The four-star hotel oozes charm and luxury, and is a treasure trove of exquisite decor, from limited edition fabrics to customised furniture and paintings by Christoff Debusschere.

The onsite Bar 1802 also pays homage to the Caribbean roots of the author and features a variety of rums, while the hotel's restaurant, Le Grand Dictionnaire, lies just across the street and serves small plates that mix modern flavours and traditional French techniques.

Hôtel Les Plumes

10 Rue Lamartine, 75009
+33 (0) 1 55 07 88 00
lesplumeshotel.com
Metro: Cadet

Inspired by the parties thrown by Monsieur Alexandre Dumas and named after his birth year, Bar 1802 has more than 700 rums for patrons to choose from. © Christophe Bielsa, Agence Webcom

The Juliette and Hugo bedroom at Hôtel Les Plumes. © Hôtel Les Plumes

The 35 rooms inside this playful hotel are each themed around famous literary lovers – think Victor Hugo and his mistress Juliette Drouet, or George Sand and Alfred de Musset. From love notes printed on the bed linen to author silhouettes in the dining room and traditional staff uniforms, this tasteful boutique hotel is imbued with all the romantic charm of nineteenth-century Paris. Perfect for a weekend getaway.

Le Pavillon des Lettres

12 Rue des Saussaies, 75008
pavillondeslettres.com/en
+33 (0) 1 49 24 26 26
Metro: Saint-Augustin, Miromesnil

Interiors at Le Pavillon des Lettres are classically French, elegant and modern, while the hotel's 26 different rooms (a reference to the 26 letters of the alphabet) are each dedicated to a famous author.

Pavillon des Lettres is full to the brim with literary fascinations. Provided by Pavillon des Lettres, © David Grimbert

Including B for Baudelaire, S for Shakespeare and Z for Zola, words from the works of each writer are stencilled onto the walls of the corresponding room, while their works are provided on the bedside table ready for some late night reading.

Hôtel Pont Royal

5–7 Rue Montalembert, 75007
+33 (0) 1 42 84 70 00
hotel-pont-royal.com/en
Metro: Rue du Bac

Located among the charming streets of the Saint-Germain-des-Prés district, the five-star Hôtel Pont Royal is a real treat. Gorgeously grand with a Michelin star restaurant, the hotel has the added cachet of having welcomed Albert Camus, Jean-Paul Sartre, Simone de Beauvoir, Françoise Sagan and the Fitzgeralds through its doors (you'll find photos of the hotel's famous clientele hanging in the grandiose lobby).

The Signature bar is also open daily and includes bespoke cocktails which pay tribute to the writers who enjoyed a tipple or two inside the very same bar, while the rooms on the upper floors boast superb views as far as the Eiffel Tower.

Right: *Hôtel Pont Royal opened in 1923 (pictured here in the 1930s).* © Hôtel Pont Royal

Below: *Hôtel Pont Royal in the present day.* © Hôtel Pont Royal

La Librairie Paris Boutik

12 Rue Caffarelli, 75003
+33 (0)1 75 43 29 26
parisboutik.com
Metro: Filles du Calvaire

Right in the heart of the Marais district, La Librairie Paris Boutik looks like a simple bookshop from the outside, but step inside and you'll find a stylish apartment with every kind of home comfort. Sleeping up to four people, the apartment comes with a kitchen, refrigerator, bathroom and – the *pièce de résistance* – more than 4,500 books lining the walls. With a vast selection ranging from paperbacks to hardbacks, biographies and novellas, there are plenty of reading lights to help illuminate those midnight page turners.

INDEX